FROM KABUL TO MANAGUA

SOVIET-AMERICAN RELATIONS IN THE 1980S

FRED HALLIDAY

90-814

PANTHEON BOOKS • NEW YORK

Library of Congress Cataloging-in-Publication Data

Halliday, Fred.
From Kabul to Managua.

Bibliography: p.
1. United States—Foreign relations—Soviet Union. 2. Soviet
Union—Foreign relations—United States. 3. World politics—
1985–1995. 4. Gorbachev, Mikhail Sergeevich, 1931– . 5. Bush,
George, 1924–   . 6. United States—Foreign relations—1989–   .
I. Title.
E183.8.S65H36   1989   327.73047   89-42656
ISBN 0-394-57310-2
ISBN 0-679-72667-5 (pbk.)

Display typography by Stephanie Bart-Horvath

Manufactured in the United States of America

First American Edition

CONTENTS

ACKNOWLEDGEMENTS

This essay develops themes explored in some of my earlier books, most notably *Threat from the East?* (1982) (published in the USA as *Soviet Policy in the Arc of Crisis*) and *The Making of the Second Cold War* (1983). It has benefited greatly from discussions which I have had over the last few years with colleagues and students in the International Relations Department of the London School of Economics, and from the seminars held by the Transnational Institute, Amsterdam and Washington.

I owe a special debt to Bob Borosage, then Director of TNI, who first suggested that I write on the Reagan Doctrine, and to Neil Belton, Maxine Molyneux and Francis Mulhern who have gone over the manuscript and made many helpful comments. Among many others who have, through discussion, suggestion and criticism helped me to develop these ideas I would particularly like to thank: Victoria Brittain, Amalia Chamorro, Joy Hackel, Michael Klare, Saul Landau, Margot Light, Christopher Coker, Dev Murarka, Jim Paul, Dan Siegel, Jonathan Steele, Geoffrey Stern, Joe Stork, Peter Utting, Achin Vanaik, Harold Wolpe, Michael Yahuda.

Part of Chapter Two was first published in *Monthly Review*, February 1988, and Chapter Three originally appeared as a Transnational Institute Issue Paper, entitled *Beyond Irangate: The Reagan Doctrine and the Third World* (1986). I am grateful to both MR and TNI for permission to reprint these materials.

Fred Halliday, London, January 1989

INTRODUCTION

This is an exploratory essay on the most crucial aspect of contemporary international security, Soviet-US rivalry in the third world. It focusses on the varying policies and ideologies produced by each of the great powers to conduct that rivalry, and the illusions which these have generated. The chapters that follow will examine these policies in their own right: they have, however, developed and are perceived within a broader context of cultural and political change. Since this is a work addressed primarily to a general audience, not one confined to specialists in international relations, it may be appropriate to begin with some summary observations on how that broader context relates to the subject of this investigation.

The 1980s were a period of signal deterioration in international relations, of Cold War between the great powers, internationalized unemployment in the developed capitalist world and immiseration in the south, as well as, at a more ideological level, of resurrected, designer, Social-Darwinism masquerading as enterprise and freedom. The cultural climate in the developed world has been marked by mass narcissism and historical amnesia: this has nowhere been clearer than in the belief that we are living in a world of one, ever-freer, 'modern' and universal political culture, with an increasingly and beneficially unified political system. Under the pretext of providing a more realistic and up-to date culture this ideology suppresses and rejects alternatives, especially those of a critical or radical nature. If there are reasons for accepting that the world has become more integrated during these years, trends in communications, economics and the management of global problems providing some evidence of this, there are also powerful reasons for recognising the inequities within this unification, and the contrary, fragmentary processes. During the decade the gap between the world's richer and poorer countries has widened, a divide which in strictly economic terms has been compounded by the new methods that advanced capitalism has developed to enhance itself, never short of innovation at someone else's expense: these include the

1

internationalization of sex–tourism, the dumping of toxic waste in the third world and the destruction, for northern use, of vast areas's of the south's ecology.

Within the developed capitalist economies themselves, there has been much talk of breaking down economic barriers and economic integration. The point is not that such a process is an illusion, but that it is taking place through a growing concentration of power, an epidemic of monopsony that is focussing power in fewer and fewer hands. Moreover, if this internationalization and mobility is true of some of the factors of production, mainly capital and technology, it must be starkly contrasted with the increasing immobility of another 'factor', namely labour. The advanced economies, which for centuries and without invitation occupied and plundered the third world, have in their post-imperial rectitude seen fit to make south-north labour flows as difficult as possible: freedom of movement for some contrasts with constriction for others. The alternative in each case, of planned allocation of resources on the basis of internationally determined needs, is thereby excluded. If this is obvious in Europe, where the introverted meta-patriotic market of 1992 is looming, it is equally evident in the abandonment by the USA of the commitment to provide a refuge for the poor of the world, at a time when US financial markets have become more international than ever before: the Statue of Liberty could, with some justice, be moved to the banks of the Rio Grande. As for Japan – a country which has, as much as any other major capitalist power, visited violence and exploitative interference on its neighbours, through the pillage of China and Korea and more recently in the brothellization of much of South-East Asia – it has never permitted immigration in the first place, with the exception of the viciously subjugated community from Korea.[1]

At the level of culture, both in its political and more strictly aesthetic dimensions, there has been an effloresence of par-ticularisms, many of them of the meanest and most historically blinkered kind. In the developed capitalist countries this has involved the inanities of the mass 'heritage' industry, often vaunting the quasi-totalitarian concept of 'community', pervasive racism and chauvinism towards newer immigrant groups, the dypsomaniac excesses and populist thuggery of international sporting occasions and in the USA and Japan, religio-nationalist intoxication in various forms (born-again Christianity, Shinto-ism). The third world itself has been awash with indigenous conflicts and ideological regressions of its own: from the self-destructive sirens of Islamic fundamentalism, which has done more than any imperialist assault from without to divide the Muslim world, to the growth of Hindu and Buddhist chauvin-isms in South Asia and the ugly spread of communalism and ethnic conflicts across much of Asia and Africa: in the Lebanon, Punjab, Sri Lanka, Philippines, Sudan and Burundi.

The 'second' socialist world has, of course, fared little better: one of the most commendable aspects of the now discredited 'old thinking' was its stress on internationalism, on fraternity between states of similar outlook, on equality between ethnic groups within nations, and on the imperative, inherited from the better side of the Enlightenment, to adopt a critical and where appropriate corrosive attitude towards the presumptions of one's own national culture and history. The advent of greater openness and pluralism has lifted the sluice gates on a tide of nationalistic frenzy and hatred, both within states (the USSR, China, Rumania, Yugoslavia) and increasingly between them. Along with many other commendable if inadequately implemented aspects of the modernizing programme repre-sented by traditional communist parties (exclusion of religion from public and political life, emancipation of women, curbing of private appropriation, planned economic development, soli-darity with the third world) this commitment to internationalist understanding appears threatened in the current, in most other respects positive (if belated) rethinking of the socialist model underway in the USSR, eastern Europe and China. The lift-ing of political controls has revealed that in these countries nothing has 'stagnated' more than nationalist myth.

This carnival of division and prejudice, while feeding on factitious history, has been compounded by a denial of real history, of the past causes of present problems and trends. The developed countries have forgotten too easily that for the first half of this century and before they attacked or occupied much of the third world almost at will, enslaving whole peoples, violating national and human rights on a global scale: the justified indig-nation of the British public at Ayatollah' Khomeini's death threat against the writer Salman Rushdie needs to be complemented by awareness of Iranian indignation at the fact that on two occasions in this century Britain, in league with its ally Russia, invaded Iran and that in the early 1950s it conspired with the USA to murder Iranian officials and overthrow the elected government of the country. It is part of the political culture of the 1980s to indulge in disavowal, a kind of post-imperial self-righteousness, when such issues are raised: it is evident in American discussion of Vietnam and Central America; in European white-washing of empire and of its racist culture; in the Japanese euphemization of contentious issues, to a degree that would put even the British ruling class to shame, and, in the case of their school textbooks, the outright falsification of history. The militaristic inebriation that gripped Britain during the south Atlantic war was a fitting expression of this globalized virus, as was the exultation in the USA at the 1986 bombing raids on Libya, in which dozens of civilians were killed. The death of the war criminal Hirohito in 1989 provided the Japanese, who have temporarily foresworn militarism, with the occasion for indulging their own imperial fantasies. At a time when there is strong public support in the USSR for a memorial to the victims of Stalin's repression, one can only wonder how long, if ever, it will be before monuments to the victims of colonialism are erected in the capitals that directed it – in Paris, London, Brussels, the Hague, Berlin, Rome, Madrid, Lisbon, Washington, Tokyo.

An essential accompaniment of this solipsistic political culture has been the belief in a new, cosmopolitan 'modernity'. This ideology, far from being universal, reflects selected values of some of the richer states in the world, and presents a range of options that are specific and exclusive. Much that is good in the past is rejected, not least a sense of history itself. Alternative definitions of what 'modernity' might constitute, of the ethical, technical and political options opening up, are removed from discussion. The components of 'modernity' can be organized as much for hierarchy as for democracy – as is most evident in the field of media ownership. At the same time, the spread of information technology, the fetish of the age, involves a further confirmation of the dominance of English at the expense of the other 4,000 odd languages on this earth. In countries like Spain and France, but also Britain, the cult of 'modernity' is saturated with a reverence for competition and 'enterprise', an officially

4

sanctioned greed that has exacerbated the gaps between rich and poor and reintroduced mass beggary onto the streets of western European capitals on a scale not seen since the 1940s. In addition to flaunting a rejection of caring and compassion at home, the political culture of 'modernity' involves a turn away from concern with the third world and with that range of issues – development aid, underdevelopment, solidarity, purposive social transformation – that marked much of the left culture of the 1970s. The most notable exception to this trend was the success of Bandaid, the mobilization to provide aid to the third world set in motion by Bob Geldof in 1985: yet despite its enormous humanitarian success, the material result of Bandaid, $70 million, was a pittance compared to the decline in real terms of north-south aid transfers and to what developed countries and their corporations were taking from the third world in various forms, not least debt repayments and declining terms of trade. Similarly the widespread support for ecological campaigns such as Greenpeace has been able to do little to impede the destruction of the rivers, forests, seas and atmosphere of the planet.

Anti-third-worldism has become a hallmark of this version of 'modernism' in the modish 'realism' of the formerly left-wing intelligentsia in the developed countries.[2] In Europe we find erstwhile supporters of the Vietnamese and Chilean revolutionary movements now singing the praises of the USA and denouncing their former allies, paralleling the recourse to irrationality and archaism in art and literary criticism: admiration for empire and 'Christian' values, a reverence for Edward Elgar and John Betjeman. In the USA there is a squalid mood, epitomised by erstwhile 'New Left' writers sneering at their former associates, entranced by Wall Street and retrospectively validating the war in Vietnam. On one issue above all, where the US government had a central role to play, that of Palestine, the majority of the US intelligentsia adopted a timid conformism, proferring 'understanding' to the Israelis, the dominators who had their own national state, and 'outrage' to the Palestinians, the victims, who did not. More than in any other developed country, this trend was associated with a penitent embrace of national ideology, a confected 'Americanism' that denied the rich history and radical potential of the country.

This political renegacy has been strengthened by a diffuse

coarsening of cultural attitudes to the third world. In regard to the countries of the south as much as towards the poor at home, it has become common to blame the victims, for their lack of initiative and enterprise. New role models are now in play. In the USA this degeneration reached its apotheosis in the figure of Rambo, a cataleptic mass murderer inflated into a national hero. In Britain there has been a parallel cultural trend, a resurgence of colonial nostalgia, nowhere more evident than in the insidious recidivism of the nomenclature of Indian restaurants: the *Moti Mahal* (The Pearl Palace) and the *Nur-i Jahan* (Light of the World) of two decades ago have become *Bengal Bertie's* and *The Last Days of the Raj*. No erotic drama now seems legitimate unless it is set on a plantation or culminates under a *punkah*. Japanese political leaders, less restrained in expressing racist attitudes, have openly proclaimed the inferiority of other, and especially black, peoples. Perhaps, if these processes continue, we can look forward to soap operas about the perpetrators of colonial genocide, to restaurants called *Coolies*, *Petit Colon*, *Le Pied Noir*, and *Banzai*, and to wine bars evoking the ambience of the slave trade – *Houseboy*, *The Middle Passage* or just *Chains*.

These packaging of modernity, and the attendant hostility to the third world are an essential backdrop to what might, on its own, appear to be a separate and welcome development, the spate of great power negotiations on third world issues. It is tempting, but premature, to argue that these have brought an end to the rivalry between the socialist and capitalist systems, and hence to their rivalry in the third world. The general impression at the end of the 1980s was that a new era of reconciliation had begun. The year 1988 was, with considerable justice, hailed as a year in which peace broke out throughout much of the world. The period of negotiation and 'new thinking' that has followed Gorbachev's emergence raised many hopes: it also contains uncertainties, above all for the third world.

It was asserted by many, from Gorbachev to Thatcher, that this turn of events marked the end of the Cold War. As I have discussed in another work, the term 'Cold War' can mean two different things.[3] In the sense of a period of acute conflict between east and west, involving confrontation and an intensified arms race, then it is certainly the case that the Second Cold War ended in 1985–1987. In the broader sense, of a rivalry between

two contrasted social and political sytstems, the historical competition that has been the fulcrum of world politics since 1945,
the Cold War remains very much in force. Nowhere is this more
evident than in Afghanistan.

In the late 1980s both the USSR and the USA have argued
that they were encouraging compromise in third world conflicts,
and a disengagement by external forces – including themselves.
Soviet writers talked warmly of there being 'No losers' in regional
settlements. In reality, such assurances were not confirmed in
the countries concerned. In Afghanistan, the Geneva agreement
of April 1988 led to a one-sided implementation: the Russians
withdrew their forces by 15 February 1989, the west (particularly the USA and the UK) and Pakistan took no notice of
the agreement and continued to supply the Islamic counter-
revolutionaries with weapons. The result was that when the
Soviet forces had withdrawn a new phase of the Afghan war,
an intensified civil war, began: no-one in Afghanistan doubted
that there was a continuing quest for victory, on the part of the
guerrillas and their external supporters.

It was an irony indeed that in the middle of February 1989,
when the western world was united in outrage at Islamic fun-
damentalist calls for the death of the writer Salman Rushdie,
protagonists of that very same fundamentalism should, in the
guise of 'freedom fighters', be mustering at the gates of Kabul,
incited by the the whole of the western world and brandishing
missiles supplied by Ronald Reagan and Margaret Thatcher.
Few bothered to ask what the 'Islamic state' propounded by
these *mujahidin* entailed. The supporters of this movement were
everywhere – normally desk-bound newsmen posturing for the
cameras in swat hats and Pathan shawls, English public school
boys entranced by a John Buchanesque world without females,
US adventurers and veterans of Indo-China eager to wreak
vengeance on the USSR, and perhaps also captivated by the
Afghan practice of mutilating the corpses of their victims, as GIs
did in Vietnam.[4] If western implementation of the UN agreement
on Afghanistan was anything to go by, there was to be no truce,
and no common ground, in the conflicts of the third world.

The role of the western European states in this process
was on the whole collusive. It was part of the success of the
new, less provocative, US interventionism and of the turn away

from serious concern with the third world that on some issues US policy was received so indulgently in Europe. It was noteworthy, for example, that the social-democratic parties of western Europe, when in power, did little of substance to help Nicaragua resist US pressure: Mitterrand and González soon trimmed to the etiquette of the Atlantic club. The US invasion of Grenada in 1983 occasioned some criticism from Britain, but this, in part motivated by concern with the proprieties of the Commonwealth, soon passed. In fact, there had been considerable collaboration in third world covert action and 'proinsurgency' policy between the USA and its European allies: between the USA and France against Libya in Chad, between Holland and the USA in organizing revolt in Surinam, between the USA and Britain in providing arms to the Afghan *mujahidin*, just as, in South-East Asia, there was Sino-US collaboration in Cambodia. When the USA sent its naval forces into the Persian Gulf in 1987, European ships joined in, a spurious 'peace-keeping' operation reminiscent of Lebanon and Korea, thereby contributing to an escalation in the war and to its prolongation for several months more. When the US Navy shot down an Iranian civilian airliner in July 1988, killing all its passengers and crew, the Europeans were mute. The countries of the EEC made much of their desire to develop a common foreign policy; their most signal attempt to do so, the Venice declaration of 1980 on the Arab-Israeli dispute, petered out, and none of the major EEC states were prepared to risk a clash with Washington on this issue.

Despite the passing fashions of the late 1980s, neither east-west rivalry nor the political challenge of the third world can go away. As was demonstrated so clearly in Afghanistan, there will be winners and losers in third world conflicts, from Cambodia to Angola and Nicaragua, and the course of these disputes is to a great extent still formed by east-west rivalry. This book has been written as a preliminary contribution to understanding this interrelationship and to ascertaining how the USA and USSR came to the turning point of the late 1980s.

Fred Halliday   London 1 March 1989

THE BIPOLAR CONTEST

In the late 1980s there was an unforeseen and unpredictable development in east-west relations. After more than a decade of confrontation – what has been termed the Second Cold War – the USSR and the USA began to negotiate bilaterally on a range of issues dividing them, particularly nuclear weapons. At the same time, in direct talks and in discussions with third world allies and opponents, they promoted negotiations on around a dozen third world crises, some of which had been raging since the 1970s, some from earlier periods: thus if the tensions in Cambodia, Afghanistan, the Persian Gulf, the Horn of Africa, Angola, Chad, Western Sahara, and Nicaragua dated from the mid- and late 1970s, those of Korea and the Arab-Israeli dispute had rather longer pedigrees. No-one could be sure where these discussions would lead and whether they would achieve settlements of the conflicts involved. What *was* evident was the great powers' apparently new interest in promoting negotiations about these conflicts, at least in part so as to reduce the dangers that third world conflicts posed to their overall global relationship.

Despite certain precedents, this trend towards negotiation on third world issues marked a break with earlier patterns of US and Soviet policy in the third world, and was subsumed by the broader shift in east-west relations characteristic of the late 1980s. As with arms control, so with negotiation on the third world; this was a reciprocal process: if resolution of some or all of these crises could contribute to a lessening of east-west tensions, the general course of Soviet-US relations would evidently have a considerable impact on how and whether these specific, local, conflicts were to be managed. The process was also a risky and uncertain one. If the new US-Soviet dialogue had positive consequences in many respects, it also involved new uncertainties: the political opening-up of the USSR created new dangers of instability, especially in eastern Europe; the US and the USSR, for all their negotiation, still saw their role in third world crises in competitive if not wholly adversary terms. The decline of Cold War II in the late 1980s therefore appeared to alter, but not abolish, the terms of conflict that applied during the forty years since the onset of the first Cold War. A brief overview of those four decades may make those terms more explicit.

Interlocking Contests: Nuclear Weapons, Third World Conflict

Two issues above all have underlain the rivalry between the USA and the USSR that has dominated the world after 1945, and which has made the international system that emerged from World War II a bipolar one. The first of these issues has been the arms race, and predominantly, if not exclusively, the nuclear arms race. This has represented the competition of the two great powers in its starkest form, both in the continuously – increasing destructive potential it produces, and in the symbolism which possession of such weapons has contributed to international power in the contemporary epoch: if the USSR and the USA are 'super' in any sense, it is in their unrivalled ability to annihilate.

The second bone of contention has been policy on conflict in the third world, an area that in 1945 was predominantly under colonial rule and which now comprises over 120 independent states. The third world has, above all, been a region of strategic uncertainty and flux. World War II drew clear boundaries in Europe, allocating the majority of states to one or other political and economic system. This allocation held, at least for four decades. In those countries where oppositions sought to alter the prevailing arrangements, established forces, without the country and within, blocked any transitions to the rival system: in the east in Germany (1953), Hungary (1956), Czechoslovakia (1968) and Poland (1981); in the west in France and Italy (1946–1948), Greece (1947–1949), and Portugal (1974). In the east it was easier for states to alter their external strategic allegiances (Albania, Yugoslavia, Rumania), for those in the west much easier

10

to vary their domestic political orientations (Greece, Spain): but while some states moved to greater independence, the cores of both blocs were maintained in place. No state made a complete transition from the Soviet to the US alliance system.

In the third world no such delimitations were stabilized: indeed, while in 1945 the summits of Yalta and Potsdam settled the division of Europe, boundaries in the Far East remained highly contested, down to 1949 with the Chinese revolution, and through to 1954 with the Korean and the first of the Indo-Chinese wars. Since then, with over 140 conflicts, costing over twenty million lives, the third world has remained an area of conflict within and between states, one in which the USA and the USSR have repeatedly been involved.

These third world conflicts have taken different forms – wars of independence from colonial rule, social revolutions against independent régimes, national and ethnic conflicts between third world peoples, and inter-state wars. They have had many causes and permit of no single description. They certainly cannot be seen simply as products of the Cold War. There is little substance to the argument that the USA and the USSR have deliberately fostered third world conflicts: their involvements have not been a way of fighting out, in a less precarious arena, the hostility which nuclear weapons and the post-1945 settlement prevent them from discharging in Europe. Much discussion in the early 1980s saw third world conflict in terms of 'proxies' and 'clients' of Moscow or Washington. This was a simplification, for Cuba as much as for Israel or South Africa. Yet though their origins may be independent of Soviet-US rivalry, such conflicts have inevitably drawn the two great powers into their field of force, presenting both opportunities and threats. Thus if Moscow and Washington *have* in many ways exacerbated these conflicts, it is important to be clear about how this has worked.

Asia, Africa and Latin America have not been frozen in the political and strategic mould that was imposed on Europe, and have therefore allowed for little of the certainty and mutual agreement of spheres of influence that characterised the post-Yalta settlement in Europe. If resistance to colonialism provided one cause of such conflict, that factor has largely been superceded; the overall incidence of third world wars did not decrease when colonialism ended.[1] Third world conflict continued, thus drawing the great powers into a succession of internal and regional disputes.

Three problems above all have confronted the great powers in the third world in the post-war period. The first has been to identify and then regulate the relationship between the two main areas of competition themselves, that is, between the nuclear arms race and rivalry in the third world.[2] The second has been the management and limitation of third world conflict and of its impact on the great powers. The third, the focus of this study, has been the development of strategies and ideologies to guide and legitimise policy in the third world.

Nuclear competition and third world rivalry have frequently been regarded as quite separate questions, products of different dynamics, and open to quite separate policy responses. In the press and in political debate, the two issues are, therefore, often treated discretely, and as alternative rather than complementary focal points of international tension. East-west does not, apparently, intersect with north-south. Yet as the strategists of both sides sometimes indicate, there is a much more complex interaction between these two. If nuclear weapons are one component, symbolic and real, of power in the world, influence in the third world is another: states which have lost ground in one domain are tempted to recuperate or compensate by increased emphasis upon the other. The adherence of both Britain and France to 'independent' nuclear deterrents is, in part at least, accounted for by the fact that those forces constitute a substitute for lost empires. Equally, possession of power in one sphere entails pursuit of it in another. This was evident in the greater US interest in nuclear superiority following the third world setbacks of the 1970s, and is clear in the degree to which both powers have felt threatened in their bilateral nuclear relations by third world crises.

At the same time, both the USA and the USSR see nuclear weapons as useful not only in deterring a straight exchange between themselves, but also as levers in third world crisis situations. The USSR, which has in general been in a position of strategic inferiority vis-à-vis the USA since 1945, has never menaced Washington in a crisis situation; but during the 1956 Suez invasion, it did make threats against Britain and France. The USA, on the other hand, has used nuclear threats of varying degrees of explicitness in a number of third world crises, most notably during the dispute over Cuba and the Soviet missiles in October 1962 and the Arab-Israeli war of October 1973. During the Korean War the USA sought to intimidate the enemy by dropping dummy nuclear weapons on North Korea. Moreover, there has always been a possibility that tactical nuclear weapons could be used in third world conflicts themselves, as a means of compensating for conventional weaknesses, and of demonstrating resolve to the other great power. The emergence in the 1980s of nuclear technologies offering higher accuracy and lower yields has made such selective usage a degree more feasible, as the January 1988 Pentagon report on *Discriminate Deterrence* recognised, with its discussion of selected, limited uses in conflict situations.

There are, of course, other and even more direct connections between these two dimensions of international conflict. The expenditure of the developed countries in both blocs on armaments constitutes a net detraction from the resources available to third world countries to resolve the economic problems that underlie much of the turbulence they experience. Both blocs have increased the destructive potential of third world states by many degrees through the sale or donation of weapons, whether such supplies are seen as part of east-west conflict or not. Both the USA and the USSR measure events in the third world as to how they will affect their overall prestige and strategic position, and in terms of the challenges posed to their security. For the USA, this process of recognizing the salience and in some cases priority of third world issues has been a disturbing one, at times leading to alarmism and inaccuracy – overstating the impact of any specific development, and trying, in a conventional way, to ascribe all change in the third world to Soviet influence. Ronald Reagan made such alarmism one of the hallmarks of his bid for the Presidency in 1980. The USSR, for its part, has counted the cost of its third world involvements, which peaked in the 1970s, and this concern has encouraged greater accommodation with the USA.

Managing Global Rivalry

The relationship between the nuclear arms race and third world policy is, therefore, a reciprocal one, involving far more reinforcement and mutual stimulation than is conventionally believed. This interaction in the late 1980s has driven the USA and the USSR to address the second broad concern that they share more systematically than hitherto, i.e. to explore ways of regulating and controlling third world conflict as part of their overall relationship. If the 1945 summits at Yalta and Potsdam focussed almost exclusively on Europe, those of the late 1960s and onwards combined negotiation of the arms race with discussion of specific third world conflicts. The first climax of this process was the May 1972 Moscow summit: Nixon and Brezhnev signed the SALT-I (Strategic Arms Limitation Treaty) agreement and, simultaneously, sought to evolve a code of conduct for dealing with crises in the third world, the Basic Principles of Relations Between the USA and the USSR.[3] (See p.171) At the same time, the USA sought to use the attraction of SALT-I and of increased economic interchange with the USSR to enlist Soviet support for a compromise settlement in Vietnam, thus enabling Washington to withdraw its forces. In this process of comprehensive negotiation, the two sides tried to barter agreements and concessions in the field of nuclear weapons, with understandings, of a more or less explicit kind, on third world situations. The era of 'linkage', the term applied by US strategists to this process, had begun.

'Linkage' as an explicit bargaining tool turned out to be of restricted use. The 1972 Basic Principles were too loose, and too liable to varying interpretations, to bind the behaviour of either side: their main effect was to provide both Washington and Moscow later in the decade with an argument for accusing the other of undermining détente. The USA saw Soviet support for guerrilla and revolutionary movements in the third world as a violation of the 1972 code of conduct: the USSR, in the person of Brezhnev, argued that no such code could be used to justify the maintenance of injustices in the third world. The USSR also denounced several US actions as violations of the principles, not least Nixon and Kissinger's flight to Tehran immediately after the Moscow summit to authorize CIA aid to Kurdish opponents of Moscow's ally Iraq. Under the umbrella of the 1972 SALT agreement, which made an allout nuclear exchange less likely, both the USA and the USSR were able to play a more active role in the third world. The middle and late 1970s were a period of unprecedented upheaval and conflict there, breaking a fragile equilibrium of state alignments that had endured since 1962, and the consequences of this were evident in both Soviet and US policy. Indeed, with the spate of fourteen third world revolutions between 1974 and 1980 détente as a whole was undermined[4]: in a grim vindication of the reciprocal interaction of Soviet-US nuclear competition and third world conflict, events in the third world were to prompt a new upsurge in the arms race. Never was the connection between the two so evident. In the 1980 American elections the Republican responded to the third world revolutions of the late 1970s by calling for a restoration of US nuclear superiority. *Pax americana* in the third world required a nuclear advantage. On the Soviet side the Brezhnevite strategies of nuclear buildup and third world advance were presented as two parts of an increasingly favourable 'correlation of forces' on a world scale.

Developments in the 1980s sustained this reciprocal interaction. In the period up to 1985, during the first Reagan Administration in Washington and the incumbencies of Brezhnev, Andropov and Chernenko in Moscow, Soviet-US relations were at an impasse on both issues – on the one hand, a heightened arms race and a lack of substantial progress in negotiations on arms control, on the other rivalry and mutual recrimination over the third world, epitomised above all in the crises of Afghanistan, Grenada, and Central America. In 1985 relations began to move beyond this impasse. Immediately after Reagan's second inauguration in January 1985, bilateral talks on regional issues commenced. This process was then accelerated by the advent of Gorbachev to power, in February 1985, and by a shift in the orientation of the second Reagan Administration towards the search for some common ground with the USSR. The culmination of this process came with the summits of December 1987, in Washington, and May 1988, in Moscow: at these encounters, as at the meeting between Nixon and Brezhnev in 1972, both the nuclear *and* the third world issues were tackled. Neither side talked now of 'linkage' or of general codes of conduct: both asserted that improved relations between them presupposed progress in both domains, and searched for agreements on specific third world conflicts. Movement and concessions in one sphere could be met by comparable changes in the other;

diplomatic movement on Afghanistan or the Gulf war could be matched by shifts in the field of nuclear negotiations as much as in another unstable situation in the third world. Thus both the confrontational early part of the 1980s and the somewhat more accommodationist second part demonstrated a continuing inter-action between the nuclear and the third world arenas.

Strategy and Ideology

These flurries of competition and accommodation were not just reactive: they took place against a wider background of changing ideas and strategies in Moscow and Washington them-selves about how to pursue a third world policy consonant with overall strategic goals, and in particular about how to handle the third world in the context of Soviet-American rivalry. After the 1950s, both the USA and the USSR evolved theories or doctrines for analysing the third world and formulating policy towards it. However apologetic and mythical some of these 'doctrines' were, they nonetheless served important functions in justifying to domestic audiences of, in both cases, a rather isolationist hue, their respective initiatives in the third world. They explained why their governments were involved there at all, and legitimised, or purported to legitimise, in the eyes of other states the interventions of the great powers in third world crises. That these theories changed as much as they did reflected both the difficulties and failures which the foreign policy orthodoxy of any one moment encountered, and also the persistent need felt by both the USA and the USSR to play a role in the third world and to manage, to their strategic advantage, the changes and upheavals taking place there.

It is these ideologies that constitute the third major set of questions pertaining to Soviet and US policies in the third world, and their analysis takes up much of the subsequent discussion in this book. On the US side, the ideologies of third world policy have been framed in a series of presidential 'Doctrines': it is an index of the importance that successive administrations since 1945 have, despite appearances, attached to the third world that every elected US president, except Johnson, has enunciated a third world doctrine of this kind. Yet even Johnson had in practice his own 'Doctrine', as his commitment of half a million men to Vietnam indicated. On the Soviet side, such policies have been formulated by the CPSU leadership, at Party Congresses and in official journals, in an evolving array of theories about the kind of social change that is possible and desirable in the third world, and on the connection between these and the Soviet-US relationship. Distinctive approaches can be associated with, respectively, Stalin, Khrushchev, Brezhnev, Andropov and Gorbachev. Elaborated at greater length than US Doctrines, these theories have had comparable purposes – to meet domestic requirements, to respond to changing realities in the third world and, as much as in the American case, to adapt policy in the face of not a few unpleasant surprises.

In the 1980s two sets of ideas, in particular, dominated the approaches of the great powers to the third world, and were designed to address both the character of change in the third world, and the place of this within the overall rivalry and interaction of east and west. In the USA, there emerged a set of ideas and policies loosely referred to as the 'Reagan Doctrine', which, well prior to the use of this label in 1985, constituted in practice a reformulation of US third world 'security' policy. In the USSR, official thinking had, for two decades or so, focussed on the possibilities of progressive change in the third world, and in particular on the promotion of change within states that had gone through a degree of revolutionary or at least radical nationalist upheaval. Increasingly, however, this broadly optimistic approach gave way from the second half of the 1970s onwards to a more cautious evaluation of the prospects for social transformation in the third world, and to a more reserved view of the place of third world upheaval in the overall course of US-Soviet relations. Revision of Soviet thinking began well before 1985. But the irony was that in the first half of 1985, just at the moment when in the USA the more activist and crusading Reagan Doctrine was being explicitly formulated, this substantial rethinking of Soviet thinking came into the open, under the influence of newly-elected General Secretary Gorbachev. If in the 1970s the Soviet Union had appeared to be gaining ground in the third world as a result of the upheavals taking place there, the reverse was true of the 1980s, a change reflected and in some degree formulated in the contrasting third world orientations of Reagan and Gorbachev. As accounts both of change and of how to respond to and channel that change, the third world ideologies of Washington and Moscow in the 1980s offer an illuminating and contrasting set of ideas, designed as they were as much to affect reality as to explain it.

SDI and LIC: The Acronymic Return of Karl von Clausewitz

The discussion that follows charts the evolution of Soviet-US conflict in the third world during the 1980s and the attendant evolution of strategic ideologies in both Moscow and Washington. Behind both policies, and their ideological formulation, there lies a recurrent, intractable but unavoidable problem, a fourth major nexus linking the nuclear and third world spheres, namely that of pursuing military and diplomatic initiatives in the third world while maintaining nuclear peace. If nuclear weapons have in one sense made wars between major powers much less probable than they were prior to 1945, they have also pushed the USA and the USSR towards ways of trying to circumvent this obstacle, towards re-establishing the link, identified in classical form by von Clausewitz, between military power and political purpose. In a sense, both the USA and the USSR have sought, in the face of potential nuclear catastrophe, to 're-Clausewitzianize' international relations. This has, in the field of nuclear weapons, led to the formulation of theories of limited or selective nuclear usage, and, since 1983, to the revival of ideas of strategic 'defence' as championed by Reagan: the Strategic Defence Initiative, if it provided a credible defensive umbrella for US military and some civilian resources, would constitute such a solution, and make nuclear weapons usable for political purposes. Moreover, weapons are to be considered as instruments of policy not just when actually used but also when accumulated in an arms race: this is why the nuclear competition itself was seen by many strategists in the west as an instrument of policy against the USSR, in that it placed intolerable burdens on the Soviet economy and forced it to concede ground, in the nuclear and third world fields.[5]

The pursuit of a new Clausewitzian link is evident not only in new dimensions of the nuclear arms race. Equally, both world powers have sought to promote and benefit in the third world from forms of limited conflict that would advance their interests while not risking all-out nuclear war. Thus in the 1950s, 1960s, and 1970s the USSR and China envisaged forms of guerrilla combat that did, precisely, re-establish the Clausewitzian link and enable war to be used as an instrument of policy in the nuclear age. Guerrilla war was, *par excellence*, a form of military conflict in which political goals, and political means, played a dominant role: political advantage compensated for military weakness. On its side, the USA began from the early 1960s to develop politico-military theories of counter-insurgency, that, first tested in Latin America and Vietnam, were to evolve into the Low Intensity Conflict doctrine of the 1980s, a theory of limited combat embodying both the suppression of revolution through allied states and the promotion of anti-communist upheaval from below. The self-styled Clausewitzians within the US strategic community, most notably Harry Summers, rejected LIC, on the grounds that it failed to see the conventional, inter-state, element in third world conflicts. But LIC itself was indeed another Clausewitzian attempt to make force politically applicable. The dominant strategic trend of US thinking in the middle and late 1980s was, therefore, a resurgence of Clausewitzian concerns, in both the nuclear domain (SDI) and in that of third world combat (LIC), two means of prosecuting conflict in a situation of great power rivalry that escaped the constraints of nuclear annihilation.

Challenges to Bipolarity

This bipolar, or US-Soviet perspective was challenged, however, not only by the gains or losses of the two main protagonists, but also by their own difficulties in controlling the actions of others. Beyond their own strategic rivalry, the two great powers have had to contend, in the third world as much as within their alliance systems, with the spread of political and economic movements that fall outside their direct control. There is little doubt that since 1945 as an overall trend the world has become less strictly bipolar, less dominated by two major states. The USSR failed to maintain its influence over China, over much of the Balkans, and over many of the non-communist third world states it initially patronised and supported, most strikingly Indonesia and Egypt. The USA encountered fewer serious challenges of a political or military nature from within its main alliance system, the case of France under de Gaulle in the mid-1960s being a limited exception; but the industrialized countries that have been so pliant in the strategic field were increasingly a challenge to the US domination of the post-war economy, and saddled the USA with the paradox of undisputed and indeed growing military power and declining relative economic strength. While Washington's main strategic rival, the USSR, was not a major economic challenge at all, Western Europe and Japan certainly were. In the third world, moreover, the USA suffered several direct political challenges from within its alliance – in China, Cuba, Vietnam, Ethiopia, Portuguese Africa and Iran especially – and found its ability to influence third world states repeatedly contested. In 1988 the paradoxical climax of the Reagan Presidency was that at the very moment when its leverage over the USSR was perhaps greater than ever before, Washington was unable to achieve its declared aim of unseating General Noriega, ruler of the small dependent state of Panama. While locked in their bipolar rivalry, both the USSR and the USA have had to face the rise of third world nationalisms that they cannot easily respond to, or ignore.

To recognise this reduction of great power influence is not, however, to accept that the world has become in any full sense multipolar, or that the power of the USA and the USSR has in every respect become less than it was two or three decades ago. In the first place, the two great powers remain far and away the most important states in the world, as their strategic and diplomatic activity demonstrates. No third bloc or state has emerged to challenge them. Japan and Western Europe are important economic forces, competitors in some domains with the USA and superior in levels of income and technological dynamism to the USSR. But they have avoided converting this economic strength into a distinct political and military capability, preferring to retain the protection of the USA. Even in economic terms there are significant respects in which the USA, for all its troubles, retains world leadership. Facile assertions of a 'lost' US hegemony overstate the reality. The US economy is by far the largest and most attractive in the world, as the flood of European and Japanese investment into it in the late 1980s attested; the dollar remained the predominant currency of international trade, giving it the 'inordinate privilege' that de

Gaulle castigated two decades before; US fiscal and budgetary policies continue to play an influential role in determining macroeconomic trends throughout the industrialized countries. Criticism of US economic policy in Western Europe and Japan usually rested not on a plea for less 'hegemony', that the US should become the equal of its partners, but on the premiss that the USA had the ability and therefore the obligation to pursue an alternative, more responsible, policy.[6]

In the 1960s and 1970s there was, equally, speculation about the rise of a new third world bloc, represented by the founding of the Non-Aligned Movement in 1961 and of the Group of 77 in 1964: by the late 1980s these had, respectively 101 and 129 members, most of them third world states.[7] But for all the exertions of these two parallel groupings to alter the balance of international economic and political relations, they demonstrated, as much as anything, their collective weakness in relation to the great powers, and their own lack of internal cohesion. The campaign for a New International Economic Order launched on the wave of enthusiasm following OPEC's success in 1973 achieved none of its stated goals and was, by the early 1980s, a stalled campaign, in practice as dead as the League of Nations: impatiently rejected by Washington, politely but ineffectively endorsed by Moscow. The calls for maintaining a nuclear-free third world rang somewhat hollow when one of the founders of the NAM, and the chairing country from 1983 to 1986, itself possessed nuclear weapons, namely India. Equally pertinent, however, was the lack of cohesion among the third world states: in economic terms, they paid scant attention to the NIEO preferring, with the New Industrialising Countries, to seek increased bilateral trade with the developed world, and treated the goal of economic co-operation between developing countries as though it had little practical import. For all the talk of interdependence, and appeals to both blocs, third world countries acted on the premiss that their main hope lay in changed priorities in the west. Political relations between third world states also belied NAM's assumption of a common interest. NAM was paralysed over Vietnam in the late 1960s, and divided again by the Vietnam-Cambodia conflict of 1978–9. As the colonial conflicts receded, new forms of inter-state war became more common. The result was that the latter issue, and

21

in particular the Iran-Iraq war, itself an ominous harbinger of possible future inter-state wars in the third world, fractured NAM during the 1980s and reduced its political credibility: division and inaction within, lessened effectiveness without. If the third world as a whole was, therefore, ineffective and divided, the power of individual large third world states – China, India, Brazil – while far greater than in the 1940s and 1950s, still brought them nowhere near the status of the two great powers, or even close to the strategic-economic position of other major industrialized countries.

In the late 1980s, therefore, four decades after the division of Europe and the commencement of the final unravelling of colonialism, the world remained in many respects a bipolar one. It was therefore especially relevant that Moscow and Washington were looking for ways to turn their hegemonic positions to collaborative ends, and, in words at least, to justify these in terms of the interests of the world as a whole. In so doing the two powers rejected the implicit assumption of much liberal thinking on the international system, that the bipolar system was an evil and that the greater the multipolarity in relations between states the better. There were those who pointed out that the international economic system had functioned best, up to 1971, when the US acted as a paramount power. There were others who saw in the multipolar spread of nuclear weapons a threat to the security of the third world. The growth of autonomous inter-state and inter-ethnic conflicts in the third world, as in the wars between Vietnam and Cambodia, Iran and Iraq, suggested that a degree of joint action by the two great powers might, in some circumstances, be preferable to a self-reproducing destructiveness in the third world itself.[8]

On the other hand, in both the USA and the USSR, there were many who opposed the assumption by their respective states of a hegemonic role, either because it involved them in unwelcome military risks and casualties abroad, or because the economic costs of a global military role were too great. There was in both hegemonic capitals much talk of ungrateful allies and thankless tasks. From 1985, the USSR was intent on concentrating its efforts on internal economic restructuring or *perestroika*, and in reducing its third world commitments and exposure. The USA was able throughout the 1980s to maintain its budget and balance of payments deficit only because of the continued willingness of the industrialized western states to accept dollars and invest in the USA, in a continuance of de Gaulle's 'inordinate privilege'. Nonetheless, despite the efforts of many third world and some developed countries to reject them, and despite considerable reductions in their hegemony, the USA and the USSR remained the twin centres of world power, and continued to compete over nuclear weapons and the third world. This is what made the summits of 1987 and 1988 and the attendant bilateral negotiations so important, for the international system as a whole as much as for the two states concerned. That they both faced continued challenges and failures in their foreign policies, competitively and jointly, did not detract from the enduring power that both retained. This was the power that was applied throughout the 1980s, with varying degrees of justification and effect, to the crises of the third world.

THE THIRD WORLD IN THE 1980s: REVOLUTIONS AND THEIR ALTERNATIVES

Revolutions are international events, in their causes and in their consequences. If revolutions in general have done as much as war, nationalism or economic change to shape the modern world (1789 and 1917, in particular, playing this role) the impact of third world revolution has been one of the formative processes in the postwar era. In that period over two dozen states in the third world have experienced political upheavals of a socially revolutionary character, ones in which a change of political system has been accompanied by radical social and ideological change, a significant degree of popular mobilization and violent conflict between opposing forces. Many of these have been directly associated with challenges to colonial rule (Vietnam, Algeria, Angola, Mozambique, South Yemen). Others, however, have been directed against independent régimes that had avoided direct colonial domination (China, Ethiopia, Afghanistan, Iran) or against post-colonial régimes, implanted from outside at an earlier period (Cuba, Nicaragua, Grenada). All had, however, a nationalist and international character in that they were in part directed against some form of external domination or link and, once the new state was established, sought to use nationalism as a means of mobilizing their populations and enforcing greater state control over their territories. All of these revolutions, too, had international repercussions, in that they promoted their new ideas and sought allies abroad, and provoked alarm and pre-emptive hostility from neighbouring states and from the great powers. Whatever the role of international factors in the *causes* of these

revolutions, there could, therefore, be no doubting their international *effects*.[1]

Revolutions and the International Dimension

Revolutions have such significant international repercussions for
several reasons. The violent overthrow of established political
and social systems and their replacement by another is not necessarily the sole means of change in third world states. In the third
world, as in many more developed countries, dictatorial political
and social systems have, under appropriate circumstances, been
replaced by more democratic systems through gradual or at
least less antagonistic processes. If in the 1970s some such
non-revolutionary transitions occurred, as in Greece and Spain,
during the 1980s transitions to more democratic political systems
occurred in a variety of third world states, most notably in
Latin America. Such transitions may avoid the enormous cost
in human life and social dislocation associated with revolution.
At the same time, such transitions can occur only under special
conditions, and even then they usually involve a substantial level
of mobilization and of suffering amongst the dominated classes
before the old order is replaced. In many cases, however, such
an outcome is not possible. Where non-revolutionary transitions
are resisted, and the ruling group prevails against political
opposition, then the prospects of revolution increase, as the
only available means of challenging a dictatorial system. Such
has been the fate of many states in the third world since
1945, as it was earlier of many of the developed countries –
Holland, England, the United States, France, Russia, and Italy
included. It has, moreover, been these revolutionary upheavals
rather than the more gradual transitions that have focussed
international attention and acted, in particular, as poles of attraction for forces in the east-west conflict. The impact of
China, Korea, Vietnam, Cuba, Angola, Afghanistan and Nicaragua on Soviet-US relations since the late 1940s is evidence
enough of this.

Revolutions occur when two kinds of cause coincide: the
weakening of the old régime, and the mobilization of the previously dominated sectors of the population. International factors
have always played a role in facilitating revolts against foreign

domination by weakening the hegemonic powers. This is especially true of great international wars. The first such global conflict, that of the French revolutionary wars between 1792 and 1815, produced revolt not only in France's Caribbean dominion, Haiti – the first successful social revolution in the colonial world – but also, by greatly weakening the Spanish state, led to the independence of much of South and Central America in the 1820s. The First World War, the next global conflict, destroyed the Russian, Austro-Hungarian and Ottoman empires, and in so doing enabled the creation of new states in the Arab world and Eastern Europe: the war also provided the final push for the release of the oldest of colonial controls in Europe, that of England over Ireland. Prior to World War II, however, the colonial rule of the major western European imperial states over the countries of Asia and Africa remained almost unchallenged, as it had done since the middle and late nineteenth century. Hitherto *all* colonial revolts there had been defeated. It is only since 1945 that the hundred-or-so states of Asia and Africa that once appeared so securely and permanently part of the western European empires have acquired independence, or that social revolutions have become possible within them.

This process, now virtually so complete that it is taken for granted, was neither anticipated nor peaceful. It was a paradox of the post-war decolonization that it was those powers who were on the victorious side in the war who then proved unable to maintain their hold on third world colonies: Britain, France, Belgium, Holland, the USA. The most tenacious were the colonists who had remained neutral in World War II and might by that token have appeared most vulnerable, the Portuguese. This outcome, however, points to an underlying common thread in the post-war retreat from formal empires, namely the degree to which the Second World War, in exhausting the victors as well as crushing the defeated, gave a world-wide impulsion to decolonization. Britain and its colonial associates emerged victorious but debilitated from World War II; London quickly ceded to India, in 1947, what it had to be forced to grant to Ireland in 1921, after World War I. The lesson of World War II, as of World War I and of the Napoleonic wars, was clear: that a principal factor in the decline of imperial hegemonies is the weakening of dominant

26

powers. At certain moments, these states for a combination of economic, military and political reasons, become unable, despite victories in the major conflict itself, to sustain what had previously appeared impregnable.

The weakening of imperial powers was not, however, sufficient reason for decolonization. Equally important were the factors impelling the subjected peoples to revolt, and to organize themselves more effectively than in earlier periods of their history. The Second World War provoked upheavals in many countries and these prevented successful reassertions of external control: in Vietnam, Indonesia, Egypt, amongst others. During the war powerful nationalist and, in some cases, communist movements had developed in Asia and the Middle East. The very demonstration effect of rising nationalism and revolt had its impact on countries where imperial authority had hitherto been unchallenged. In guerrilla warfare, subjected peoples found a new, sometimes effective means of increasing the pressure on occupying powers. The imperial states rarely 'granted' independence to the former colonies: it had to be wrested from them, in many cases though protracted and sanguinary wars that left their mark on the countries concerned long after the imperial armies and their flags had departed. In Vietnam, Algeria, Angola and Mozambique millions died before the colonial power was forced to retreat.

The process of decolonization was, in its barest terms, one in which an imperial power transferred power to a local nationalist régime. This in principle finite procedure was not, however, to mark the limits of how third world conflict would affect international politics as a whole. It was accompanied by three other processes that complicated the colonial and post-colonial periods and deepened their international repercussions. These bound the conflicts of the third world permanently and more closely to the east-west conflict developing in Europe. The first of these processes was the frequent combination of a nationalist movement with social revolution, evident in such cases as Algeria, Vietnam and Angola. This meant that the nationalist forces threatened the existing balance of east-west relations. The second such process was of war *between* third world states, onto which an east-west dimension was superimposed. Two of the most important of these conflicts exploded in the late

1940s, as colonial power was withdrawn: the Indo-Pakistani and the Arab-Israeli. While these were to endure and re-explode over the ensuing years (there have been three Indo-Pakistani and five Arab-Israeli encounters), there were to be others: Ethiopian-Somali (1977–1978) and the Iran-Iraq (1980–1988) wars amongst them. While drawing on animosities and disputes with roots in the colonial and pre-colonial past, these most recent disputes took their most virulent form after revolutions in the larger of the two states involved (Ethiopia in 1974, Iran in 1979).

The third important process was the entry into the third world of the USA and the USSR, the two states that had emerged as great powers from World War II but which did not have what, in the classical European sense, could be regarded as colonial empires, with the exception for the US of its colonies in the Philippines and Puerto Rico. If they encouraged the withdrawal of the colonial powers, they also exerted themselves to draw the third world into their own bloc-systems. In the decades of third world upheaval since 1945 the initial clash of colonial power and national resistance movement has been overlain by these other dimensions of conflict: social and political antagonism, with international repercussions within states; conflict between independent third world states; and Soviet-US rivalry in the third world as a whole. The withdrawal of the western European empires has created the context for new, menacing and destructive forms of conflict in much of the third world, and provided new opportunities and challenges for both great powers.

The course of revolutionary upheaval in the third world can be seen in terms of three waves, three periods of delimited duration, when revolutionary challenges broke the power of established régimes. What is striking about these waves is the fact that, simplification aside, they are identifiable periodically, suggesting amongst other things that the conditions for successful revolutions are as much international as internal. In other words, both external encouragement to revolt and the almost indispensable weakening of hegemonic power on an international scale would seem to be preconditions for the success of specific, internally generated revolts.

Revolutionary rhetoric may exaggerate the degree to which

revolutions repeat themselves and, more specifically, the degree to which the essential domestic preconditions for revolution – political, social and economic – reproduce themselves within different countries. Simple calls for world-wide revolution have never borne fruit as their exponents have hoped – whether those of the French Girondins in 1792, of Lenin at the founding of the Comintern in 1919, of Lin Piao in his celebration of people's war in 1965, of Che Guevara with his call for 'two, three, many Vietnams' in 1966, or of Khomeini with his call to the oppressed peoples of Islam in 1979. But history is nonetheless replete with examples of revolutionary waves, of periods when, in countries far apart geographically, revolutionary upheavals coincide, for reasons that go beyond mere chance. There were six political revolutions in Europe in 1648. The period 1760–1800 has been called the age of the 'Atlantic Revolution', because of the great transformations on both sides of the ocean, most noticeably in the USA and France. 1848 brought conflagration throughout much of Europe. The years 1905–1920 saw revolutions in a score of countries that had avoided outright colonization, but were subjected to partial modernization by capital – China, Persia, Russia, Egypt, the Ottoman Empire and Mexico. The end of World War I permitted revolutionary insurrection in many parts of Europe – successful in Russia, defeated in Germany, Hungary and Italy.

In the post-1945 period there was one such wave in the years 1944-1954 (Albania, Yugoslavia, China, Korea, Vietnam, Bolivia, and many unsuccessful ones in, among other countries, the Philippines, Iran, Malaya and Guatemala). A second postwar wave came in the years 1958–1962 (Iraq, North Yemen, Congo, Cuba, Algeria). After 1962, and despite many upsurges in the third world, no state fell to revolutionary forces, with the single, remote case of the British colony of South Yemen in 1967. But from 1974 to 1980 there was a third revolutionary wave, covering no less than fourteen countries, across the whole geographical span of the tropical south: Vietnam, Cambodia, Laos in Indo-China; Afghanistan and Iran in Central Asia; Ethiopia in the Horn and Zimbabwe in the south of Africa; the five Portuguese colonies – Angola, Mozambique, Guinea-Bissau, Sao Tome and Cape Verde; and, in the western hemisphere, Grenada and Nicaragua.[2]

The 1970s: Triumph of the Political

One aspect of this revolutionary wave was of particular importance: in most cases the triumph of the revolutionary movement
had come about through a form of combat generally regarded
as outmoded, namely guerrilla war. In some periods, when its
importance and prospects are overstated, guerrilla war generates
a special myth as 'the' unorthodox solution to a conventional
impasse. This was true for allied strategists aiding anti-Nazi
forces in Europe during World War II, for much of the left in
the third world in the 1960s, and again in the 1980s for the right.
In each case the 'myth of the guerrilla' overstated the capacities
of those involved. However, if it is prone to exaggerations, at
other times guerrilla warfare is written off prematurely. In the
late 1960s, with the failure of *focista* struggles inspired by Che
Guevara in Latin America, and the apparent containment of
guerrillas in Africa and South-East Asia, it was commonly
asserted that successful guerrilla warfare was no longer feasible,
given the effective political and military counter-measures it
provoked.[3] Yet in the final reckoning, eleven out of the fourteen
revolutions of the 1970s triumphed in this way; they won through
not by victory in the field alone, but by a combination of military
pressure *and* a political weakening of the opposing state.

Guerrilla warfare is a politically flexible instrument: irregular
warfare against an established state can be used by left or right.
What distinguishes guerrilla warfare as a form of struggle is
not, however, merely the form of such unorthodox military
campaigns, but the political dimension that shapes them: the
process of weakening the power of the established state through
political means. Where, as has usually been the case in the
postwar world, most of the states challenged by guerrilla war
have themselves relied on external support, the straining of this
external link, the weakening of the hegemonic power's determination, has been a key to the success of guerrilla opposition. If
this was true for Kuomintang China in 1948 and Batista's Cuba
in 1958, in the 1970s this undermining of the internal and
international conditions of domination played a key role, not
least in Vietnam and Nicaragua, where the withdrawal of US
support, direct in the first, mediated in the second, played an
important part in hastening the end of the Saigon and Managua

régimes respectively. The successes of guerrilla war in the 1970s therefore rested to a considerable degree upon the ability of these weaker forces to make the hegemonic power abandon its previous commitment to a given third world state. It was changes in Washington and Lisbon, rather than outright military victories, that made possible the guerrilla triumphs of Indo-China and Lusophone Africa. Without the guerrilla challenge there would have been no change of policy in the metropolis: but the goal of the military campaigns was as much to weaken the political will of the enemy, and embolden resistance within the metropolis, as to gain territory or other advantages in the field.[4]

The revolutions of 1974–1980 were an international, tricontinental phenomenon: the impact and significance of this third wave of revolutions were far greater than the consequences for the individual countries themselves. It is apparent that some were inspired by the international climate of the times and by the lessons, real or imagined, of conflicts often far away: thus Nicaragua was encouraged by Cuba and Vietnam, Grenada by the reported significance of Iran. Of perhaps equal importance was the fact that the Vietnam war had weakened the credibility of the USA as a hegemonic power in the third world. It is not necessary to argue that, had it not been for the defeat in Vietnam, the USA could or would have intervened directly in any other third world crises during the mid-1970s, to see that the international weakening of US hegemony contributed to some of the revolutionary outcomes of these events. In the Angolan crisis of late 1975, Castro decided to send tens of thousands of troops to Africa only after judging, correctly as it turned out, that the US Congress would not authorise US military action against the expeditionary forces. Had the US chosen to halt *Operation Carlota* on the high seas or in the air there is little Havana or Moscow could have done about it.[5] In Iran, the belief that the USA was qualifying its support for the Shah, and had become more critical of human rights abuses among its third world allies, encouraged the early phases of the revolution in 1977–8, even if the ultimate beneficiaries, the clergy, cared little for such issues. Equally, the willingness of the USSR to provide military backing to third world resistance movements (in Vietnam, Lusophone Africa) and of Cuba to do so in Central America constituted another enabling feature of this third revolutionary wave. There is no need to seek for a single cause of these fourteen upheavals, or to deny the very great differences between them, to see how certain general international factors contributed to the outcome.

The 1980s (i): Democratisation

It was these international factors which, compounding local causes, produced the revolutionary conjuncture of 1974–1980. The consequences of the 1974–1980 conjuncture were, equally, of broader and international character: these results to a considerable extent explain the very different course of events in the 1980s, and the very different responses to the third world evident in the USA and the USSR. The record of political change in the third world in the 1980s presents a marked contrast to that of the previous decade. On the one hand, there was an increased incidence of change *without* revolution, of democratisation, or at least of transition from dictatorial to more open, democratic, systems. In the 1960s and 1970s there had been numerous cases where forms of democracy had been abolished by military intervention with US approval if not always involvement: in Brazil in 1964, in Chile in 1973, in Pakistan in 1977. In all three the military received support, at least after the event, from the USA.[6] In the 1980s, however, the trend was reversed. While the military ended a democratic interlude in Bolivia (1977–1980), elsewhere democracy returned. This was especially so in Latin America where in several countries military régimes ceded to civilian administrations: in Peru (1980), Argentina (1983), Uruguay (1983), Brazil (1985). In Mexico the one party monopoly of the PRI was being eroded, as the contested presidential election of 1988 made clear.[7] In each case this democratic opening reflected a combination of internal pressure and a shift in the international climate. In a number of other third world countries too there was substantial and to a degree successful pressure from below, for democratisation leading to changes in state form: in Haiti, South Korea, the Philippines, Pakistan. In the largest Arab country, Egypt, the death of Sadat in 1981 introduced a much more liberal political climate under his successor Husni Mobarak. In Thailand, military dictatorship was replaced by civilian rule in 1985. In Pakistan, the death of Zia in 1988 led to the first comparatively free elections in over a decade.

The opening of these countries to greater democracy, qualified and precarious as it often was, rested upon a set of internal and external preconditions. The dictatorial state had to have come to a point where it could no longer credibly retain power. The pressure from outside had to be such that its pre-existing hegemonic support was eroded. Yet in many cases the political conditions of the crisis were not such as to produce this outcome. In Paraguay and Chile military régimes held onto power: elsewhere, adjustments were made by the ruling group and its international supporters to counter the opposition and prevent substantial change. The successful formula was to maintain the core institution of the régime, the armed forces, and prevent its erosion while introducing a new political leadership, the latter being in some cases a prisoner of the former: it was tested in Sudan, Philippines, Haiti and South Korea, and was also the formula that, it was hoped, would succeed in Pakistan and in Turkey.

The 1980s (ii): Revolution Contained

However, the shift towards greater civic and political liberties was matched elsewhere by an at least equally pervasive blocking of the revolutionary challenges that continued to be posed to established régimes: indeed, if democratisation was one tendency, the other prominent feature of the third world in the 1980s was the containment of social revolutions. The third wave came to a halt in 1980, as the second wave had in 1962. In the 1980s as much as in the 1970s there were substantial social upheavals and great loss of life in many third world states: but in no case in the nine years 1980–1988 did a revolutionary movement come to power, as fourteen had been able to in the period from 1974–1980. This apparent stabilisation was not because all the possibilities of social revolution in the third world had been exhausted or because democratic alternatives existed: in Paraguay, El Salvador, South Africa, Namibia, Chile, Palestine and elsewhere there were movements committed to overthrowing established dictatorial or discriminatory régimes. Nor did this blockage occur, in cases where revolt threatened US allies, for the reason that had been so significant in the middle and late 1960s – namely the direct intervention or threat of US force;

such overt interference had characterised the years from 1965 onwards, following the full-scale US entry in 1965 into the Dominican Republic and Vietnam. During the 1980s the US did intervene directly in some cases: in Grenada, Lebanon, Libya and the Persian Gulf. But these were limited operations, falling short of protracted commitments of ground troops and avoiding significant casualties. Rather, the successful prevention of social revolution reflected two other developments which, in their combination, were to leave their mark on much of third world politics during the decade: in sum, the onset of Cold War II and the crisis of third world revolutionary régimes.

The third world played a much more central role in the origins of Cold War II than in those of Cold War I. If third world conflict was important in the late 1940s and early 1950s, it played this role in a subordinate, largely secondary, manner. It is true that the first major clash of the Cold War was the Azerbaijan crisis of March 1946, when British and US pressure forced the USSR to withdraw its forces from northern Iran and abandon its substantial political allies inside Iran to the Shah's mercies: with the US and British-backed coup of 1953, the military dictatorship in Tehran was secured. Yet from 1947 onwards, the focus of the Cold War was on Europe and particularly Berlin. Only in 1949 did the centre of conflict shift to the Far East, with the triumph of the Chinese communists in 1949 and the outbreak of the Korean war in 1950. Even this latter conflict, by far the bloodiest of the First Cold War, was seen in the west above all in global terms, as a displaced response by a Stalin frustrated in Europe, rather than what it was, a national-revolutionary conflict within a third world country.[8]

In the Second Cold War, the situation was very different. At the inter-state level Europe was stable, its borders and social orders sanctified by the 1975 Helsinki Agreement. A scare about 'Eurocommunism' had passed by the late 1970s. Western and particularly US alarm about the USSR focussed on two questions: the alleged Soviet superiority in nuclear weapons, and the Soviet role in conflict in the less developed world. The USSR was, it was claimed, gaining ground at the expense of the USA, and 'pushing Washington around'. The most prominent examples of this Soviet 'expansion' in the third world were Afghanistan, Angola, Cambodia and Nicaragua, but around these there developed a wider mythology of a new Soviet presence in the third world which was responsible for much of the turmoil there and constituted a strategic threat to the USA. Thus the Soviet role in the Arab-Israeli war of October 1973, the Ethiopian-Somali war of 1977–1978, in the Shaba uprisings of 1977 and 1978 in Zaire were all incorporated into this image of Soviet expansion. The result was that with the change of political climate in the USA in the late 1970s and the election of Ronald Reagan in 1980, US foreign policy concentrated on opposing Soviet influence and, of equal importance, on challenging the third world gains which the USSR had made in the 1970s. The revolutionary wave of 1974–1980 set the scene for the Reagan Doctrine of the 1980s.

If for the USA the third world was the site of a new offensive strategy in the 1980s, the situation of the USSR was rather different. For Moscow, the revolutions of the 1970s represented an ambiguous development. On the positive side, they enlarged the number of states friendly to the USSR, and willing to provide some diplomatic support. The number of countries where the USSR had a military influence also increased. On the other hand, the developments of 1974–1980 imposed new costs on the Soviet Union. All of these states were in economic difficulties and looked to the USSR for support that it could give only to a limited degree. Many of these states engaged in policies at home and abroad that the Russians disapproved of, on the grounds that these were precipitate and dangerous, and that they encouraged social resistance. Most important of all, perhaps, was the price that the USSR paid for its third world allies in terms of its relationship with the USA. Inside these countries, US support for local oppositions was imposing a heavy burden on the USSR and their local allies. In bilateral terms, the issue of the Soviet role in the third world, actual or purported, was used to justify the US arms buildup of the early 1980s and to impede progress on a range of strategic issues. The more cautious Soviet attitude to third world revolutions evident in the 1980s was, therefore, in part a function of the difficulties and risks inherent in revolutions themselves, and in part a function of the overall calculation of Soviet interests in a period of Cold War confrontation with the USA. This re-evaluation of third world commitments, to be discussed at greater length in Chapter

4, was already evident in Moscow in the early 1980s: it became more explicit and far-reaching with the advent of Gorbachev to power in February 1985.

This new strategic configuration, and its impact on Soviet and US policies, was perceptible in several domains. First, the USA was enabled on a number of occasions to use direct military force in the third world, against Soviet allies, without provoking any significant Soviet response: against Syria, via Lebanon, in 1982–1984; against Grenada, in 1983; against Libya in 1983 and 1986. If the US use of force was not so significant *within* specific states, it was important in highlighting the greater leeway now open to Washington. Second, through various forms of loose alliance and *entente*, the USA encouraged others to put pressure on Soviet associates in ways that were not open to the USA itself. China against Vietnam, Israel against Syria, South Africa against Angola and Cuba, France against Libya – all played such a role in the late 1970s and early 1980s. To cast these states as 'proxies' as if they were simply acting at Washington's behest is simplistic; on the other hand, to deny the importance of the association with Washington would be naive. They attacked enemies targetted by the USA, and bore costs that Washington wished not to bear itself. Third, the USA sought to prevent revolutionary forces from coming to power, either through counter-insurgency assistance (El Salvador) or through pre-emptive management of transitional situations (Haiti, Philippines). This composite strategy demonstrated the greater resources of the USA in the third world, and the ability of the USA both to check revolutionary and to harness counter-revolutionary forces throughout Asia, Africa and Latin America.

Of all the novelties of the 1980s none was, however, more significant than the new *offensive* component in US policy, the subject of Chapter 3 of this book. In response to the earlier two waves of revolution, the USA had focussed its attention on checking revolutionary advance *and* on counter-insurgency: in Korea, the Philippines, Iran and Guatemala during the first wave of the late 1940s and early 1950s; in Latin America and Vietnam during the 1960s. In response to the third wave, such traditional policies were maintained, but the US reaction was distinguished by the attempt to go further, to undermine and destroy already established revolutionary states, both as a means of overextending the USSR and of deterring others from imitating or being assisted by such states. The assault upon third world revolutionary states and its insertion into the overarching US-Soviet rivalry was what most distinguished third world conflict in the 1980s.

A Crisis of Post-Revolutionary Transformation

This shift in the strategic situation, and the offensive initiatives pursued by Washington, placed special stress upon the newly established third world revolutionary states. Moreover, this pressure came at a time when the internal direction and potentiality of third world revolutionary transformation were increasingly uncertain.

In the 1950s and 1960s the non-European post-capitalist states, China above all, at least appeared to be pursuing a self-confident alternative path of revolutionary transformation, one that constrained foreign influence, mobilized domestic populations and encouraged other resistance forces. It was a clear revolutionary alternative to the capitalist world and minimized relations with it. In the 1980s, this insulation and self-confidence had weakened. There was, instead, a pervasive crisis within post-revolutionary societies, one that left leaderships and populations much less certain as to how to change and develop their societies. Socialist states now sought to increase relations with the world market. It was this combination of the US offensive, with the crisis of third world revolutionary development, that gave the former its particular impact.

The 1980s posed, in perhaps a sharper form than ever before, the question of how far revolutionary transformation, based on a degree of self-reliance or de-linking from the world system, can be a viable alternative strategy of development for third world states, and particularly for those that emerged from social upheavals. The wave of revolutions in the 1970s yielded a group of new states that were trying, amidst great internal and international difficulties, to implement more just and autonomous development models. Prominent amongst these were Nicaragua, Angola, Mozambique and a reunited Vietnam. Even Iran, tormented by regressive ideology and clerical dictatorship, in some respects pursues a more self-reliant model, by reducing oil exports, redistributing wealth and limiting consumer imports. Yet these experiments in transformation, and the chronic inability of capitalism to meet the needs of most of the third world, were accompanied by a crisis of the revolutionary model itself. What was, for many socialist and third world writers of the 1960s, a self-evident and practical option was no longer so straightforward. The new revolutionary régimes that emerged from the 1970s had no ready blue-print or established system of international non-capitalist support waiting for them.[9]

If this crisis was evident enough in theory, it was equally obvious in the practical domain: many of the countries that pioneered radical change and self-reliance now appeared to be diluting or abandoning it. Fashion in thinking on development, and the priorities of multilateral funding agencies such as the World Bank, reinforced this trend. Tanzania's experiment in 'African socialism' appeared to be exhausted. China, albeit unsteadily, swung to integrate itself into the international capitalist system. In 1988, Teng Hsiao-ping advised a visiting Mozambiquean delegation *not* to follow China's attempt at socialist development.[10] Even Albania was discreetly exploring commercial links with Canada, France, West Germany and Italy. Country after country that went through revolutionary upheaval in the 1950s and 1960s appeared to be in economic crisis and wracked by problems that were supposed to have been overcome: if this was evidently true in the more advanced socialist countries, the USSR first amongst them, it was equally so in third world revolutionary states. The result was that by the latter half of the 1980s virtually every revolutionary third world state, with the signal exception of the DPRK, was introducing new policies designed to accommodate to the shifting and unfavourable international situation, and the loss of momentum within the domestic sphere. In Vietnam, following the Ninth Party Congress in 1986, a new foreign investment law was introduced and the internal economy liberalised. In Laos, one of the five poorest states in the world, a cautious 'opening' began in 1982, and after the Fourth Congress of the ruling Lao Dong Party in 1986 a direct approach was made to the IMF, as state controls were relaxed. In Mongolia, the oldest of the third world revolutionary states, the influence of changes within the USSR was evident: the Brezhnevite party secretary Yumzhagin Tsedenbal was removed in 1984, and the Nineteenth Party Congress of 1986 introduced a number of substantive internal reforms; this culminated in the Law on State Enterprises of April 1988, comprising an expansion of enterprise autonomy and new accounting methods based on profit and loss. In Ethiopia, Mengistu announced in November 1988 that the private sector in industry and agriculture would now be encouraged.

In what had perhaps been the most hopeful of the third world revolutionary experiments, that of Cuba, the state pursued an erratic economic path that indicated a similar degree of crisis. After enjoying a relatively successful economic recovery in the early 1980s, Cuba entered a period of crisis as a result of falling energy prices: it had relied on reselling cheap Soviet oil at (higher) world market prices, but income fell from $500 million in 1986 to $220 million in 1987. Abrogating forms of individual enterprise encouraged in the early 1980s, in agriculture and the service sector, the Cuban government in 1987 launched a programme of recentralisation or *rectificación* that offered little alleviation of the problems the country faced. It was justified (see Appendix 4) in terms of a return to the economic doctrines of Che Guevara, whose heroic moral example was upheld as a solution to the Cuban crisis; but the record of Guevara's policies had been questionable, and had contributed much to the shortages of the latter part of the 1960s. Whether it could resolve the difficulties of the 1980s was something that many doubted, including a substantial number of Cubans, not least because this swing to austerity coincided with the promotion of foreign tourism and the resulting contrast of facilities available to Cubans and visitors.[11]

In some cases, the difficulties of revolutionary transformation reflected the direct and destructive impact of counter-revolutionary assault upon it. By 1987 Angola calculated that the South Africa- and US-backed rebellion had cost it 60,000 lives and $12 billion in damage, with no end in sight: at the same time oil revenues from Angola's exports of around 400,000 barrels a day had fallen from $2 billion in 1985 to $0.7 billion in 1987. In response, in August 1987, a new reform programme, of economic and financial 'cleansing' *(saneamento)*, was introduced to stimulate the economy. In Mozambique, the

South African-backed rebellion had produced a situation in which up to half of the 14.6 million inhabitants were dependent on international aid, large numbers were refugees, and over 100,000 people had been killed: in response to this crisis, FRELIMO in 1983 introduced a reform programme that relaxed control of farmers, and sought to reduce state direction of the economy. In Nicaragua, the attrition of the *contra* war had, by the mid-1980s, severely undermined the reform programme of the FSLN and prompted widespread discontent with the social and economic aftermath of the revolution. Their enemies were not slow to take note of the chronic problems of these states, and responded by direct sabotage, designed to exacerbate the problems of a transition to socialism, or through the more judicious enticements of aid agencies promoting the private sector and reducing welfare programmes.

The crisis of self-reliance had, moreover, been fuelled by case after case in which the very attempt to implement such a policy had led to self-induced political catastrophe within the country itself: to fratricidal in-fighting within the leaderships, as in Grenada (1983), South Yemen (1986) and Burkina (1987). In each of these cases, there was significant conflict between personalities in the leadership itself: between the New Jewel Movement leaders Maurice Bishop and Bernard Coard in Grenada, between President Ali Nasir Muhammed and Abdul Fattah Ismail in the PDRY, and between Thomas Sankara and Blaise Campaore in Burkina. But these personal and factional issues overlaid a set of differences over policy, and in particular over how far it was possible in a small, economically weak, third world state to pursue a path of radical reform. In the case of Grenada, the cautious policy pursued by Bishop after 1979 had led to a number of economic and political problems within the country, to which his opponents in the NJM leadership drew attention: their alternative, however enveloped in Marxist-Leninist theory, was an unrealistic one for a revolutionary régime, as the policy they pursued so tragically demonstrated. In the name of orthodoxy, they undermined the whole revolution, first by killing Bishop, the leader who had the support of the population, and then by imposing a coercive régime that enabled the USA to invade and claim, amidst the welcome of almost the entire Grenadan population, its most complete counter-revolutionary victory ever. In Grenada as in South Yemen, the moderate paths pursued by Bishop and Ali Nasir did indeed cause widespread resentment inside the ruling party, but in both cases this resentment crystallised into a dogmatic opposition that offered no way forward for the régime as a whole.[12]

The questions of policy and model confronting any post-revolutionary régime in the third world remained inescapable. The analytical framework of the 1960s, 'dependency theory' – developed through a critique of external domination and of the liberal illusions of interdependence – suggested that a self-reliant path and state control of international trade were viable and necessary. Self-reliance did not necessarily entail a complete severing of links with the international capitalist market, but it did involve a reduction of these ties and a limiting of such links to those areas of interaction which were of prime importance for development, and over which the revolutionary régime could assert control. The theory suggested, for example, that there could be national control of resources, a reduction in the influence of foreign states and companies, insulation from fluctuations in the international market, and a planned pursuit of new and more egalitarian social and economic goals. To a greater or lesser extent this model implied that new forms of international cooperation between like-minded self-reliant states could enhance the options for each individual state: this would occur either through alliances of third world countries, or through a new international economic system based on the socialist countries.[13]

The record of subsequent decades suggested, however, that in theory and practice autonomous development was not only more difficult to pursue than originally believed, but that it could also produce new tensions within the society concerned, making a stable pursuit of socio-economic transformation more difficult. At the economic level, self-reliance encountered several problems: limits on the size of domestic markets, scarcity of natural resources, inefficiencies protected by state subsidies. By reducing contact with the international market, self-reliant states inevitably limited their access to foreign exchange and so reduced their ability to acquire capital and technology. There were, at the same time, problems of a political nature associated with the self-reliant policy, quite apart from the embargoes, sabotage and counter-revolutionary pressure exerted by other states. Any such programme necessarily involved internal social conflict, in which the possessing classes, including those in the service sector, had ample scope for undermining the new state. The dilemmas for revolutionary states were acute: precipitate nationalisation or collectivization could spell ruin, while indecision might surrender the initiative to opponents.

At the same time, the ideological and political mobilization of populations for self-reliance could involve not only a perilous strengthening of the central state and ruling party, but also, as China, the DPRK, Cambodia and, in its special way, Iran showed, the fostering of frenzied nationalism within the population, and its almost universal accompaniment, the cult of a leader and his personality. The call for a return to 'indigenous' third world values that so often accompanied theories of self-reliance was not so easy in the aftermath of Pol Pot and Ruhallah Khomeini: it was their very 'authenticity' that cost their own peoples so dear and promoted values and practices in some ways more oppressive than those of western imperialism. On the other hand, such mobilizations, particularly over a period of years, were in many cases extremely difficult to sustain: any strategy of transformation, based on restricted consumption and a clear priority for longer-run investment, was liable to encounter popular resentment in a world where the majority of the poor, let alone of other social classes, wanted far more than the satisfaction of basic needs. The loudspeakers and TV screens of the global village and capitalism's shop-windows – from Hong Kong and Seoul to Miami – did much to disorientate the nearby revolutionary experiments.

These problems were, in some cases, greatly exacerbated by another trait of third world revolutionary régimes, namely the resort to reforms coercively imposed from above as a way of accelerating social change. All revolutions involve a combination of initiative from the top and from below, but where the former is excessive, people may develop great resistance to it. Much of the inertia and scepticism about *perestroika* among the Soviet population in the 1980s can be traced back to the terrifying, numbing experience of Stalin's forced collectivization and industrialization and his purges of the 1930s. The Great Leap Forward and the Cultural Revolution in China did much to alienate the Chinese population from the régime and from any ideal of socialism.

Many third world régimes in the 1970s, from the DPRK and Cambodia to Ethiopia, were intoxicated with revolutionary 'projects' and phrases, often laced with a fervent nationalism.

Perhaps the clearest case where this attempt to accelerate change produced a counter-tendency was in Afghanistan. Upon taking power in April 1978 the leaders of the People's Democratic Party of Afghanistan proceeded to decree substantial changes: this in a society where traditional values held sway over most of the population, where armed resistance was easily organized in the countryside, and where the ruling party, itself sorely divided, had around 10,000 members, nearly all of them in the cities, to rule a country of 15 millions. The result was that internal resistance, encouraged from abroad and fanned by PDPA brutality, grew apace. By the middle of 1979 much of the countryside was in revolt, and the régime isolated: the intervention of Soviet forces in December 1979 prevented the fall of the PDPA, but it provided neither a military nor a political solution and served to galvanise external support for the opposition. When the Soviet forces began to withdraw in 1988 and 1989 the régime appeared as isolated and internally divided as ever. Rarely can the effects of miscalculated reform from above have been clearer, or more catastrophic.[14]

In the 1980s, therefore, the accumulated internal problems of third world revolutions came to the fore. In this context a substantial re-thinking on third world revolutions began to occur, which subjected to critical examination a range of suppositions underlying earlier theories of self-reliance. Some experts now believed that semi-autarchy, in the sense of doing without international trade and capital imports, was simply not possible for small third world countries. Provided that it was possible for revolutionary states to establish an adequate measure of control over domestic and international economic activities, they argued, the maintenance of a significant level of international trade, matched by a gradualist approach to the private sector within the country, was perfectly feasible.[15] Others showed that socialist states, and others like them in the third world, could have much greater access to international finance in the post-revolutionary phase than conventional wisdom suggested.[16] Since a reliance on some degree of external finance was inevitable, the task facing such régimes was that of obtaining it on the best terms and with the fewest political conditions attached, rather than doing without it altogether.

Dilemmas of the 'Middle Road'

Reconsiderations of this kind, and the stress on a new middle road in economic and political policy, provided a much more convincing vindication of third world revolution than some earlier, more dogmatic accounts. Yet the 'middle road' of asserting state control while allowing a private sector to flourish, and taking a cautious approach to reform, generated its own difficulties. The combination of internal opposition by investors and traders and external pressure can make any middle course very difficult to follow: it is not by accident that disputes about such issues as the private sector, incentives and foreign trade, lay at the heart of the leadership crises in Grenada (1983) and South Yemen (1986), as well as providing the material for major debates in Russia and China. The reintroduction of large-scale foreign tourism in Cuba in the late 1980s provoked considerable resentment among the population. If there was a new, more moderate consensus on self-reliance, it was one that sometimes understated these problems and ignored some of the practical reasons why earlier revolutions had behaved with what appeared to be dogmatic abruptness.

A second problem with third world revolutions concerned the power of the state and the possibility of democratic control over it. Throughout the postwar period, it was taken as axiomatic in much sympathetic writing on revolutions in underdeveloped countries that 'mass' participation in decision-making was compatible with revolutionary transformation and could indeed provide an additional support to the revolutionary process. There was an element of wishful thinking here, in that an ideal of 'mass' democracy and 'participation' was upheld while the very problem of politics in the transition period, of reconciling democratic representation and state power, was overlooked in a justified revulsion against those advocating outright revolutionary dictatorships. Yet any process of radical transformation almost inevitably encountered resistance within and hostility without, and was bound to lead to a strengthening of the state and of its security apparatuses and a denial of democratic control over

44

them: the greatest popular mobilizations, in peace and war, have required central direction to sustain themselves, and such direction inevitably carries serious risks. The historical record of revolutions is eloquent enough: they mobilize populations, yet enhance the autonomous power of states; they make the state more representative of popular interests, but also strengthen its control over the population. Not to confront this problem makes it more difficult to delineate democratic spaces within such transformations.[17]

Another issue that was treated gingerly in discussions of self-reliance was that of popular attitudes and values. It was easy, but misleading, to assume that if only the masses were given their voice all would be well. No successful revolutionary leader ever believed this, though rather fewer have admitted it, Lenin and Mao being two exceptions. This problem arose particularly acutely with the issue of economic allocation – as between social groups, between different regions of a country, and between consumption and investment. Spontaneity alone could produce no clear mechanism for deciding proper balances in this domain. On a range of other issues central to social transformation, mass spontaneity and participation also led to serious problems within the revolutionary process: on the question of women's rights, where popular attitudes, including those of many women, were often of a retrograde character (in Iran and Afghanistan, but also in China and Nicaragua); on relations between ethnic groups, where traditional chauvinisms could flourish, decked out with revolutionary justifications (against 'reactionary' or 'feudal' Tibetans, Kurds and Eritreans); on attitudes to other nations (Russian attitudes to Chinese, Chinese to Vietnamese being prime recent examples). Recognition of this problem did not provide a justification for dictatorship; but it did suggest that a simple acceptance of what passed for 'popular' attitudes and values could be problematic.

Beyond the confines of the individual revolutionary process itself, there lay the difficult area of international relations: for all the talk of a new socialist community powerful enemies were many here and friends rather few. Powerful econom-ic hierarchies remained and were strengthened in the 1980s. Indeed Ronald Reagan's great contribution to the revival of Marxism was his firm reinscription onto the map of a concept that had rather gone out of fashion in the late 1970s, namely 'imperialism'. The original theory of imperialism, upon which dependency theory rested, was inadequate: the nature of international capitalist hegemony was changing, and not all contact with industrialized capitalist countries inhibited development or political independence. But there was nonetheless an enduring international hierarchy of developed and developing countries, based on economic and political factors, and ferociously defended by military means: this was at no time more true than in the 1980s, when new forms of hierarchy developed as economies were internationalized. Throughout the postwar period the gap between the world's richest and poorest nations continued to widen. Those who blamed all the problems of third world revolutionary states on a timeless 'imperialism' were deluding themselves: imperialism changed, and many third world problems were the result of internally generated mistakes, conflicts, and dogmas. But that external pressure of various kinds was, and would continue to be exerted on third world revolutions was indisputable. For all its ambiguities, the word 'imperialism' was the best available to denote this network of international relationships.

On the other hand, third world revolutionary states were forced to confront a range of problems that originated not from the enemies of socio-economic transformation in the third world, but from those friendly to it. The simplest model of self-reliance dispensed with this problem by denying that it existed – every country could look after itself. The reality was that external military and economic support, was essential for most, if not all, countries pursuing such transformations; the question of where to obtain it, and at what price, was an acute one. In the 1980s there was usually only one answer: the USSR. The military assistance provided by the Soviet Union was vital to the security of a number of third world states: North Korea, Vietnam, Cambodia, South Yemen, Ethiopia, Angola, Cuba, Nicaragua. The USSR also provided a model of social and economic organization: while it was easy to show how forms of Soviet politics or economics applied to third world states were inappropriate, the Soviet model was at least a practical answer to administrative needs. Moreover, many of the problems of third world states were caused not by imitating the USSR but by indigenous and voluntarist policy

46

mistakes (the 'ten million tons' campaign in Cuba, for example, or the Great Leap Forward in China).

What the USSR crucially failed to do was to provide an alternative international economic system within which third world states could reorientate themselves away from the capitalist world, or negotiate with it from a position of greater strength. The reasons for this failure were objective and real: the overall limits of the Soviet economy, its shortage of foreign exchange, its – in many domains – inferior technology. If the USSR provided a military and political system that enabled the post-revolutionary régimes to survive, even if these models were in some ways unsuited to the country concerned, it could not offer the kind of economic support which these countries required. The perspective of classical socialist theory that the more advanced revolutions would redress the weaknesses of the more backward, the 'law of combined and uneven development', was therefore blocked off: the developed socialist countries could not and did not provide sufficient economic or political compensation to enable the less developed to make a transition to socialism. Instead, the third world revolutions acted as a brake on the development of the more advanced. The uneveness therefore retarded the combination.

The fate of revolution in the 1980s was, consequently, an inescapably international one, a product of two processes: the impact of the Second Cold War, and the crisis of socialist development which taken together served to contain the revolutionary momentum of the 1974–1980 period and to threaten the viability of those states that had gone through radical change in that period. In the case of the smallest in scale of the fourteen revolutions of the 1970s, that of Grenada, direct military intervention by the USA reversed the verdict of the New Jewel Movement's popular triumph. In another, Afghanistan, the combination of mass resistance from below and large supplies of military assistance from the USA had, by the end of 1988, made it doubtful that the PDPA régime would survive. Throughout the two dozen or so revolutionary states of the third world problems of internal socio-economic transformation, exacerbated by political misjudgement at the top and unfavourable international conditions, had created a widespread conjuncture markedly different from that of the 1970s.

Asymmetric Conflict and World Politics

The development and outcome of the Vietnam War was characterised by 'asymmetric conflict'.[18] The Vietnamese guerrillas,
faced with a military balance unfavourable to them, sought to offset this by opening up political balances that would compensate
for their military deficiencies. Thus within Vietnam they were
able to mobilize large sections of the population for a protracted
guerrilla war, while internationally they could count on both the
indirect support of Russia and China, open up divisions within
US society and play on the weaknesses of the US economy. The
result of this drawn-out and – for the Vietnamese – very costly
strategy was the victory of 1975. This triumph for national
liberation forces in Indo-China then served to weaken the
USA's interventionist resolve as a whole, and so to facilitate the
global revolutionary conjuncture that lasted until 1980.

The situation in the 1980s was, as we have noted, markedly
different, and was characterised by a relative stalemate in the
third world. After 1980 no revolutionary movements came to
power, and while the USA was unable to reverse most of the
revolutions against which Reaganism was a reaction, Afghanistan
did represent a significant exception. As we have seen, Grenada
was another, a largely self-inflicted defeat by the New Jewel
Movement, which opened the door to Reagan in 1983: but it
was a setback of little strategic importance. Yet the stalemate
in Indo-China, southern Africa and Central America was itself
deceptive, since what it represented was not so much the freez-
ing, let alone exhaustion of the conflict between revolutionary
and counter-revolutionary forces, so much as an overall and
inevitably temporary balance: an equilibrium of asymmetry produced by the confrontation of the two forces, and of their relative
strengths and weaknesses. The key to the Reagan Doctrine was
to be found in this balance, in the way the USA on the one hand,
and its third world opponents on the other, sought to offset their
own weaknesses by exploiting the weaknesses of the other side.
Asymmetric distribution of strength and weakness, as in the
period of the Vietnam war, determined the course of the conflict.

On its side, the USA had certain major strengths. First, it had
overwhelming military capability and firepower in any potential

third world confrontation. Secondly, it had great economic strength, and was more productive and technologically advanced, and more attractive by virtue of its consumer prosperity to populations of less developed countries and those of the Soviet bloc. It could use this economic power to pour resources into military expenditure and to influence the policy of international economic bodies like the IMF against support of third world revolutionary régimes. On the other hand, the USA was constrained by factors that lessened its ability to apply the full weight of its military and economic advantages to the leverage of counter-revolution. Most important was the reluctance of US public opinion, expressed directly in Congress, to support direct, protracted or costly US military involvements in third world states. A quick *promenade militaire* in Grenada, or an air strike against Libya, was popular at home. But when it came to involvement in the Lebanon in 1983–4 US domestic support was lacking, as it was for a full-scale intervention against Nicaragua. US opinion was belligerent on some issues but not prepared to contemplate heavy casualties.

On their side, the targets of overt and covert Reagan Doctrine action were vulnerable régimes, but they could not easily be swept away, for all the military and economic harrassment to which they were subjected. They were tempered in years of war prior to the seizure of power, and they had in many cases learnt from the errors of their predecessors: the Cubans, for example, advised a number of their third world allies – Nicaragua, Angola, Ethiopia – on the need not to nationalize large sections of the economy in a precipitate manner, and on the importance of maintaining some diplomatic dialogue with the USA and US public opinion whatever the policies and provocations of the US government. These régimes came to power with considerable popular support, and while some of this was eroded by the difficulties of the post-revolutionary period, compensation could be drawn from the mobilization of patriotic support against external intervention. This was evident in, for example, Nicaragua. Secondly, despite their overall military weakness, these régimes were prepared to continue fighting against external intervention and US-backed guerrillas, even at considerable cost to themselves. The asymmetry of cost in blood so evident in Vietnam was repeated again in Cambodia, Angola and Nicaragua. Thirdly, for all Moscow's desire to compromise, these régimes could count on at least some military support from the USSR. Soviet economic aid was meagre, and official Soviet policy stressed that these countries had to rely on their own resources for their main development needs. But they were given the wherewithal to maintain their armies and to counter-attack against US-backed forces. It was hardly a coincidence that in the months prior to the November 1985 Geneva summit, which marked the easing of Cold War II, all six of the third world revolutionary states facing right-wing guerrillas launched major military campaigns against them. This global Soviet-backed offensive was a testimony to the unified nature of the conflict, of the linkage between great power confrontation and the particular local conflicts of the third world.

War, and the threat of war, played an important part in the conflict between the Reagan administration and its third world opponents. But, as in Indo-China, the decisive battleground was not so much military as political, within and between the states concerned. On the USA's side, the key issue became that of internal political opinion, in particular whether the administration could acquire the degree of domestic support needed to make continued use of its military and economic superiority. Much of the energy of the Reagan presidency, with its rhetoric of 'freedom fighters' and 'terrorists' and its exaggeration of the threat posed to the USA, was designed to mobilize support for LIC, and, if necessary, for more direct forms of US intervention. The emphasis on 'public diplomacy', the manipulation of domestic opinion, recurs throughout official US discussion of this strategy.

Among the victims of Reagan's attentions in the third world, the key question was the coherence of their own support – from their own populations, from their international allies and, by no means to be assumed or overlooked, within their own leaderships. What gave Reagan an opening was significant weakening in one or other of these three dimensions – significant popular rejection of the revolutionary régime, lessening of military and diplomatic support (as in Afghanistan), or a major division within the revolutionary leadership (as in Grenada). One of Nicaragua's greatest assets was the coherence of the Sandinista leadership. In the era of nuclear weapons, it is too quickly forgotten how far military conflict remains a product of politics, and that any use of force must be combined with appropriate political conditions to be successful. As we can now see the Reagan Doctrine, and the resistance to it, were eloquent examples of this continued politico-military interconnection.

INTERVENTION REVIVED: THE REAGAN DOCTRINE

Doctrines and Presidents: The Coherence of Incoherence

Upon entering the White House in January 1981, Ronald Reagan proclaimed his outright hostility to third world social revolutions. He linked upheaval in the South to the east-west conflict, and argued that a firm stand on the latter required an equally firm stand against the former. Reagan built up America's potential for intervention in the third world, and engaged in a variety of measures – military, political and economic – against radical states. At the same time, he sought to build a constituency for this policy at home, and promoted a comprehensive and quite successful shift of the domestic debate to the right, as demonstrated by his vice-president's electoral success in 1988. In his 1984 re-election campaign he boasted that since coming into office no state had fallen to the left in the third world, a claim that held when he completed his second term in January 1989. The policy of containment and rollback became a hallmark of the Reagan presidency.

As will be shown later, the policies subsequently associated with the 'Reagan Doctrine' were not, at least initially, the only ones to be aired in the neo-interventionist atmosphere of the early 1980s. In the aftermath of the Vietnam defeat two forms of interventionism were propounded. The first, linked to a 'strategic' school, treated third world conflict in more orthodox terms as a conflict between states, requiring direct assault and intervention against enemy countries, while the second, the 'low intensity' or 'irregular' school, regarded third world conflict as being of a novel kind, requiring new, non-conventional, approaches.[1] In the early Reagan years these two schools ran parallel to each other, but by 1984–1985 the 'low-intensity' variant had prevailed. Developed initially as a set of separate policies and threats, this latter policy crystallized in 1985 as the 'Reagan Doctrine'.[2] In his State of the Union Message of that year the President pledged US support for anti-communist guerrillas in third world states. 'We must not break faith with those who are risking their lives on every continent from Afghanistan to Nicaragua to defy Soviet-supported aggression and secure rights which have been ours from birth . . . Support for freedom fighters is self-defense'. In a speech delivered in the same month Reagan declared:

> 'Time and again we've aided those around the world struggling for freedom, democracy, independence and liberation from tyranny . . . In the 19th Century we supported Simon Bolivar, the great liberator. We supported the Polish patriots, the French resistance and others seeking freedom. It's not in the American tradition to turn away.'

After Reagan's pronouncements of February 1985 his arguments were amplified by many commentators, official and unofficial. Most prominent amongst the former was Secretary of State Shultz who, following the USA's humiliation in Lebanon, made himself the champion of this Doctrine within the administration as a whole. In a major speech to the National Defense University in January 1986 Shultz stressed the need for the USA to commit itself to support for those requesting help in third world conflicts. Perhaps the clearest unofficial exposition of the Doctrine was an article in *Time* magazine, in April 1985, by Charles Krauthammer, an editor at the New Republic. Krauthammer called for an end to the pretense that action by the USA in support of third world allies and guerrillas was self-defense or justified in international law. He called Reagan's February speech 'overt and unashamed American support for anti-Communist revolution'. This was, he said, 'a kind of ex post facto containment: harassment of Soviet expansionism at the limits of empire'.

The practical components of the Reagan Doctrine were encased in a broader package of rhetoric and declamation, a new ideological message that became the keynote of Reagan's second term. For all its vagueness and incoherence this doctrine had a clear message – of attack. In his pre-election statements in

1980, and during his first four years in office, Reagan laid greatest emphasis upon the east-west dimensions of this outlook: through polemical speeches on the Soviet system, the buildup of US military capacity, and the search for confrontation on bipolar issues, especially arms control. The term 'Reagan Doctrine' was even used on occasion during his first term, in reference to the strategic doctrine of 'prevailing' in nuclear wars, and in regard to the use of US forces in Grenada. But the explicit emergence of the doctrine had to await the second term, and in particular the special stress upon support for 'democratic' and 'free' forces around the world. The choice of this rhetoric was itself a reflection of the calculation by strategic planners in Washington that it had an objective advantage in the US-Soviet conflict as a whole, and could therefore benefit from pushing this advantage ideologically and in third world situations. A characteristic statement of this was made by Shultz in an address to the Commonwealth Club in San Francisco, also in February 1985, where he evoked a two hundred year history of US support for 'those around the world struggling for freedom and independence'.

The results of the Reagan Doctrine were substantial: in terms of interventionist expenditure and real increases in US military capabilities, in terms of the loss of life and economic disruption visited upon third world states. In certain countries, direct intervention of US forces took place – Lebanon, Grenada and Libya. For those directly affected by the Reagan Doctrine, and for those who would be its objects even after Reagan left office, the Reagan Doctrine was an ominous and costly development. In several countries, notably Afghanistan, Angola and Nicaragua, it imposed a very high price on Soviet allies. But while the real and the rhetorical effects of this doctrine were considerable, it is also necessary to set it in some historical context, and, having done so, to identify its limits.

Historically, the Reagan Doctrine was the latest in a line of 'doctrines' proclaimed by post-war US presidents in order to link third world upheavals to great-power rivalry. These Doctrines may have been woolly or misleading: yet they sought to do something precise, to justify US action outside the advanced industrial world. The Reagan Doctrine too was another answer to an enduring question: *how* should the USA respond to third world revolt? It is indeed striking that this issue, not economic philosophy or general principles of American idealism, has time and again led presidents to lend their names so firmly to a given policy. If this was true on occasion before 1945 – Monroe in the 1820s, excluding European powers from the Caribbean and South America, and thus opening the way for numerous later US interventions; Roosevelt, in his 1904 'Corollary' to the Monroe Doctrine proclaiming a US willingness to intervene in South and Central America – it has been especially so since 1945: Truman in 1947, announcing US support for the governments of Iran, Turkey and Greece, the latter the site of the only revolutionary war in Europe after 1945; Eisenhower in 1957, proclaiming US support for conservative states in the Arab world; Kennedy in 1961, promoting a mixture of pre-emptive social reform and counter-insurgency that he believed could prevent further 'Cubas'; Nixon in 1969, responding to the casualties sustained in Vietnam by developing a new policy of 'Vietnamization' and more general reliance on strong third world allies; and Carter in 1980, faced with the failure of the Nixon Doctrine in the Persian Gulf, announcing that the USA would build up its forces in the area to replace the Shah and fill the strategic gap apparently opening up between US deployments in Europe and the Far East. There was, therefore, little that was new about a US president affixing his name to yet another programme of third world counter-revolution. What requires explanation is why in the 1980s a new doctrine became possible and necessary, and why Reagan had to make a new contribution to this field. To answer this requires a summary examination of developments in the 1970s, and of the challenges and opportunities which the third world revolutions of that decade presented to the USA.

From Counter-Insurgency to Pro-Insurgency

The Reagan offensive was a response to the changing world situation confronting the USA at the end of the 1970s – a decade of considerable setbacks to which it was inevitable that the USA would in time react. Four aspects of the late 1970s situation provoked US policy-makers into a new assertion of imperial will in the third world and to the indirect interventions that Reagan endorsed: the crisis of pre-existing policies and doctrines of third world counter-revolution; the unprecedented, tricontinental, advance of revolutionary forces; the growing alarm and bewilderment within the USA about the course of world events, including third world upheavals; and, by no means least, the opportunities which the newly established third world revolutionary states presented for covert action, destabilization and even invasion.

The history of US counter-insurgency in the third world since 1945 has been that of the successive presidential doctrines, each of them an apparently more effective response to a previous setback or defeat. Yet each was itself followed by failures that appeared to undermine the validity of the doctrine when applied to other parts of the world. Thus the Truman Doctrine was followed in 1949 by the triumph in the Far East of the Chinese revolution, an enormous defeat for the USA in a country which had long been an object of special US interest, economic and emotional, and whose Kuomintang government had been granted equal status with the big four in the wartime coalition and the UN Security Council. The Eisenhower Doctrine justified a US intervention in Lebanon in 1958 but was ineffective against Cuba and its example elsewhere. The Kennedy Doctrine appeared to work in Latin America, where in the 1960s no repetition of the Cuban revolution occurred and where US covert action, amplifying the sabotage activities of the Chilean right, ensured the overthrow of the Popular Unity government in 1973. But the Kennedy Doctrine, of combined social reform and counter-insurgency, failed its biggest test in Vietnam, as did its successor policy of committing directly large numbers of US combat troops. The latter had no name, but was in practice the Johnson Doctrine. Its failure, battered home in the 1968 Tet offensive by the Vietnamese communist forces, led to Nixon's July 1969 proclamation of the doctrine of a mediated US role. Iran, Israel, Egypt and Brazil acquired enhanced regional roles. This doctrine was, in effect, to last for a decade, until the accumulation of third world defeats led to another revision of US policy and to the evolution of a new and more assertive doctrine.

The turn of events that led to this revision was, as we have seen, the spate of revolutions that rocked the third world between 1974 and 1980. The Reagan Doctrine was, in essence, a response to this third wave of post-war upheavals challenging western power from Vietnam to Nicaragua. The US reaction varied from country to country. While by far the most costly and strategically important instance was Vietnam, the full impact of this was at first camouflaged by US relief at withdrawal in 1973 and the ensuing Watergate crisis. The impact of Vietnam was, however, most evident in the reluctance of the US people to support further interventionary activities, the so-called 'Vietnam syndrome'. There is no doubt that this anti-interventionist mood in the USA had its effects on other conflicts – it made it more possible for Cuba to send troops across the ocean to defend the MPLA in Angola in 1975 from South African attack, and it contributed to the triumph of the FSLN in Nicaragua in 1979. But as the 1970s wore on, the simple anti-interventionist stance was eroded by events and by sharper debates within the USA. A new mood of panic and anger about the world became apparent: it first became visible with the debate on the Panama Canal Treaties in 1978, it remained focussed on the Caribbean in 1979, with the factitious panic over the Soviet 'combat brigade' in Cuba and the FSLN victory in Nicaragua, and it reached its crescendo with the hostage crisis in Iran, which lasted from November 1979 until January 1981.

Alarm within the USA about the third world was not merely generated by events in third world countries themselves – it combined concern about rising oil prices and the power of OPEC with a more diffuse sense of lost American power, and hysteria about a supposed Soviet superiority in nuclear weapons. The world appeared to be getting out of control, and Reagan offerred an answer. *In nuce,* his solution was twofold: a return to the pursuit of nuclear superiority, to the claim that America should be 'Number One' (as explicitly called for in the 1980 Republican Party election manifesto); and a more assertive role in the third world. Vengeance – against hostage-takers, Vietnamese communists and terrorists – was part of the mood, and through it the repressed anger and pain about Vietnam came to the surface. Only in 1983, ten years after US combat forces left Vietnam, was a memorial to the 57,000 US dead erected in Washington. The political and emotional rewriting of the war swept America, from Rambomania, to the necrophiliac obsession with MIAs, to the rather selective debate about the 'lessons' of Vietnam. There was a lot of discussion of what Vietnam 'did' to the USA, little of what the USA 'did' to Vietnam. Most important, in practical terms, was the emphasis placed by many in Washington on not allowing 'it' to happen again. While there was little agreement about just what the 'lessons' were or what 'it' was, everyone seemed hell bent on applying them this time around. Or so it seemed.

The emergence of the Reagan Doctrine was not only, however, a product of the US domestic feeling and its response to third world revolution, another chapter in the paranoid strand in US politics. It was also a response to the character of these revolutions as perceived in the USA. On the one side, the political conflicts and repressions that marked many of these upheavals were publicized in the USA and used to portray these countries as totalitarian and evil. Thus a country like Nicaragua, which did not practice widespread human rights abuses, was lumped together with Iran, which certainly did. The use by some of terrorist tactics, strictly defined, was used to discredit all who fought for liberation, and the use of terror by US allies was ignored. On the other side, policy-makers focussed upon the evident weaknesses of these régimes and the acute problems they faced in the immediate post-revolutionary period. Thus a State Department official in April 1986:

> The Soviet determination to consolidate and, where possible, extend their influence in the Third World persists. But Moscow's ability to sustain such policies is being challenged in a new way. They now confront growing indigenous resistance movements in the regional outposts of influence they established in the 1970s . . .
>
> The United States cannot fail to respond to these emerging democratic resistance movements. Our reason is simply stated: freedom for others means greater peace and security for ourselves.
>
> Our efforts to promote freedom, prosperity, and security must accommodate the differences among these regional conflicts and the conditions under which they arose. The form and extent of our support must be carefully weighed in each case. Since popularly supported insurgencies enjoy some natural military advantages, our help need not be massive to make a difference.

But our assistance must be more than symbolic: our help should give freedom fighters the chance to rally the people to their side. As President Reagan has made clear, '. . . resistance forces fighting against Communist tyranny deserve our support,' And in Afghanistan, Angola, Cambodia, and Central America, where people are fighting for national independence and freedom, we should provide support.[3]

The anterior history of revolutionary régimes – Cuba and China among them – provided ample evidence of the degree to which post-revolutionary reforms alienated part of the population and generated discontent among previously privileged groups. The overwhelming economic superiority of the west generally in output terms and in the availability of consumer goods provided an ideal means of distracting and demoralizing the populations of these states. If to this economic challenge was added that of arming and encouraging guerrilla opposition then the scope for harassment of the new régimes was enormous. Counter-revolutionaries could sustain opposition and destabilization activities only if there existed some minimal social support for such policies within the countries concerned. It was precisely this support among counter-revolutionary sectors which, in Afghanistan, Nicaragua, Angola and Cambodia the Reagan Doctrine used to promote its new offensive. The new radical states of the third world appeared to offer 'softer' targets than the more established states that had emerged from the upheavals of 1945–54.

The shift to a more assertive US policy began prior to Reagan's entry into the White House in January 1981. Faced with growing opposition at home, particularly in Congress, and with the spread of revolutions in the third world, Carter took a number of measures that departed from the liberal Trilateralist approach that he had espoused in 1977. For example, he began to extend the US military presence in West Asia, under the auspices of his own Carter Doctrine announced in January 1980, and he increased the US military deployment in the Caribbean. He initiated covert aid to the Afghan guerrillas. Overall military expenditure began to rise again in 1978, and some of these new allocations were for an enhanced presence in the areas so threatening to US power.

Whatever Carter started in the latter period of his Presidency, Reagan took much further, in substance as well as tone. Yet the Reagan Doctrine as it emerged in the second term was also a product of changes in Administration policy that had matured during the years 1981–4, through which the 'strategic' approach was replaced by the 'low intensity' or 'irregular' method. Perhaps the most influential retrospective book on the Vietnam war by a military analyst, *On Strategy* by General Harry Summers, drew two lessons above all from that experience: the impossibility of defeating the NLF in the South so long as direct attack upon its backers in the North was precluded; and, in an invocation of von Clausewitz, the need to match means to ends, to fight a war that had a political and social goal with political and social, rather than exclusively military means. The need to conduct what another strategist has termed 'offensive ground operations within the contiguous sanctuary', i.e., to hit North Vietnam rather than just the revolutionary forces in the south, was an approach that appeared to command the support of Secretary of State Alexander Haig in the early part of the Reagan Administration: thus he talked of the need to put pressure on Cuba and Nicaragua in order to push back the revolutionary forces in El Salvador. Contesting the 'strategic' approach of Summers were those who drew another 'lesson', the need to avoid large-scale direct US involvement, and this informed much of the thinking on Low Intensity Conflict. It is relevant, therefore, to look briefly at how the 'low intensity' displaced the 'strategic' approach, why it took so long for the Reagan Doctrine to emerge, and what the initial, 'strategic', policies were that were later displaced or abandoned. In summary form it can be said that the initial policy rested upon three planks, each of them based on a model of conventional inter-state conflict i.e the 'strategic' approach:

(i) *'going to the source'*, by hitting directly at the countries aiding US opponents in third world conflicts, such as Cuba, Nicaragua, Syria and Libya;

(ii) *linkage*, or compelling the Russians to abandon support for third world states and movements in return for US concessions on arms control and east-west relations as a whole;

(iii) *delegation*, the encouragement or at least tacit endorsement of strong third world states that were, for their own reasons, willing to attack Soviet allies in the third world: Israel and South

Africa, both of which invaded their neighbours during the early Reagan years, were the main collaborators in this respect.

The process of strategic rethinking and debate over the third world was a complex and drawn-out process, spanning much of the early 1980s. It was complex because it took place in many different milieux, in distinct institutions of the US state, in academic and semi-official research institutes and in what are often, with some hyperbole, referred to as 'think' tanks. It was drawn-out because it took until 1985 for a coherent new strategy to emerge. In official terms, there was a rapid revision of military doctrine: LIC was incorporated into army doctrine as early as January 1981, with greatly increased funding for counter–insurgency and special forces. In academic and intellectual circles, it became fashionable to support intervention once again. A range of reports and studies fostered a climate of aggressive interventionism. One illuminating example of this was the 1984 *Report of the National Bipartisan Commission on Central America*, usually known, from the name of its chairman, as the Kissinger Commission.

Eight Hours in Managua: Kissinger's Contribution

When former Secretary of State Henry Kissinger was asked by the Reagan Administration to head a commission of enquiry on Central America, it must at first sight have seemed a curious initiative for the then current US Government to take. Although an inveterate counter-revolutionary, Kissinger was, after all, vilified as an east coast 'liberal' and associated with the 'détente' policies so excoriated by the incumbent of the White House. He himself had never demonstrated any expertise on Central America: indeed there is not a mention of its strategic importance in the nearly 2,500 pages of his published memoirs. His conduct of the enquiry itself was hardly serious: he spent in all eight hours in Nicaragua, six of them with opponents of the régime. Even the idea of appointing a commission to advise on foreign policy was an aberrant one: after all, there existed in Washington not one but several bureaucracies devoted to the making of foreign policy (the State Department, the National Security Council and the CIA). A public commission of twelve personalities was an odd way to determine policy.

This is all true if one assumes that the purpose of the Commission on Central America was to formulate policy on Central America. The saga of the Kissinger Commission becomes more intelligible if one looks at it in a different light. The Reagan Administration was perfectly capable of developing a policy on Central America with its own resources. It had also demonstrated the ability, almost unique amongst US Administrations, of shaping its foreign policy in secret: the Irangate crisis was to demonstrate that. What the Commission served to do was to forge a bipartisan approach *within* US politics, to decide not what the USA should do in the lands between Mexico and Panama, but to cover the home front, to mobilize internal support and befuddle domestic criticism. A similar logic lay behind the appointment in the same period of a commission on the MX missile. For Kissinger himself the political purposes were equally patent: to deal himself back into the Washington game after more than seven years in the wilderness, and to have a second chance to formulate the policies that so eluded him in Vietnam. For on line after line, ponderous page after page, it is that great defeat on the battle-fields of Indo-China *and* at the negotiating table in Paris that haunts his discussion of Central America. He had lost last time. This time he hoped to win.

The analysis of the Commission is predictable enough itself. It argues that the crisis in Central America has two roots: the internal socio-economic crisis, caused by years of inequality and the impact of the recent recession; and an external crisis, the result of Soviet and Cuban involvement. Little evidence of the latter is provided but the task facing USA was, so he argued, to resolve the first, whilst meeting the second. There is a lot of hand-wringing about the terrible situation Central America finds itself in. 'We ardently wish that there were no need for a security chapter in a report on Central America, but there is.' So begins Chapter 6. The chapter goes on to identify four ways in which events in the region could pose a direct threat to the security of the USA: first, by forcing the USA to devote more resources to defending the southern approaches to its frontier; second, by creating a threat to US shipping lanes in the Caribbean – vital for US imports and for naval links to Europe in the event of a world war; third, by bringing about 'a proliferation of Marxist-Leninist States that would increase violence, dislocation, and political repression in the region'; and, fourth, by eroding the worldwide perception of the USA as a country capable of influencing events beyond its frontiers. The link between local insurgency and the USA is also made by a foreshortened account of why there is rebellion in the region. The gestures in the direction of accepting the socio-economic causes give way time and again to the unsubstantiated assertion that it is the fault of the Cubans and the Soviets.

So, the answer is clear. Aid to the Nicaraguan counter-revolutionaries should be continued. The Nicaraguan revolution itself must not be allowed to consolidate. And there must be increased military aid to Guatemala and El Salvador. The majority of the Commission members argued that aid to El Salvador should be made 'conditional' on that country's human rights record. Kissinger and two other Commission members would have none of this 'conditionality': 'We wish to record our strong view that neither the Congress nor the Executive Branch interpret conditionality in a manner that leads to a Marxist-Leninist victory in El Salvador, thereby damaging vital American interests and risking a large war.'

The superficial mildness of much of the report indicates the political purpose of its drafters. The further it goes in calling for social reform and economic aid the more it appears to meet the objections of the liberal centre in the USA, in Congress and in the Catholic Church in particular. The kind of division that occurred within USA over Vietnam must be avoided: this was above all the lesson that Kissinger learnt. He now blamed the defeat of Vietnam on the fact that the Nixon Administration was hamstrung by Congress and unable to maintain its military presence in Indo-China when revolutionary threat emerged after 1973. The first pre-condition of successful counter-revolution in Central America, one which would eventually involve US combat forces, was therefore a solid political backing at home.

The promises of money and handouts had, however, additional functions. For such programmes had been at the centre of US counter-insurgency campaigns in the third world ever since World War II. One of the first principles of such programmes was that the only way to defeat communism was to undermine it socially. The stabilization programmes of the late 1950s – in South Korea, Japan, Taiwan, the Philippines –

were based on precisely this belief in land reform as the basis for counter-revolution, a policy articulated by the exiled Polish agronomist Wolf Ladejinsky. Later, the counter-revolutionary reform model was applied elsewhere: during the Kennedy Administration it framed the measures of the Alliance for Progress, in Latin America, and the White Revolution in the Shah's Iran. Kissinger's apparent conversion to such programmes masked a deeper, unacknowledged continuity. While some of the money was for pre-emptive reforms, the majority of the funds were to flow into the hands of those who already hold power and wealth. It was, in effect, mainly a programme for subsidizing the middle classes in these countries, building up their political resolve, and endowing them with funds for the consolidation of their rule.

On its own, this strategy did not work in Vietnam, however. And it is here that Kissinger, remembering his defeat nearly a decade after the Vietnamese revolutionaries drove their tanks through the gates of the presidential palace in Saigon, evidently drew other lessons as well. In Vietnam he sought to combine diplomacy with war, to pressure Hanoi at both levels: in the end he was outwitted and defeated. The lesson to be drawn from this was that the USA had, in later US phraseology, to 'go to the source': there could be no negotiation with Nicaragua until the government in Managua was so pressed that it surrendered its goals, or was forced to allow opposition elements into the government alongside the revolutionaries. The strategy for Nicaragua that Kissinger outlined was one that would lead to the dislodging of the Sandinistas. This time 'Hanoi' had to be crushed. Whereas Kissinger allowed some power-sharing in the agreement with Hanoi worked out for South Vietnam in 1973, now no such risks were to be taken with El Salvador, the South Vietnam of Central America.

The Commission's arguments involved a number of logical twists designed to square the circle of public legitimation of US counter-revolution. One of these involved the use of the term 'democracy': time and again the Commission argued that the USA should encourage democracy in Central America. It reached the bizarre conclusion that alone of the five countries Nicaragua was moving away from it. The fact that in Guatemala, El Salvador and Honduras those who opposed the government were liable to be killed by its death squads hardly figured in the analysis; yet 5,000 at least died in this way in El Salvador in 1983 alone. Kissinger's reservation on 'conditionality' gave the lie to the whole 'democracy' argument: faced with a choice between imposing its will and respecting human rights, the USA must, he argued choose the first. Indeed the whole thrust of the report can be seen as an attempt to win support for such a policy within the USA.

The 'democracy' theme also involved some peculiar games with historical truth. Page two of the report contained a pair of quite contradictory statements about the past. The first was that it is history, together with contiguity and consanguinity, which binds Central America to the USA. But lower down the page we find a rejection, so bland in its arrogance, of the historical responsibility of the USA for what was now occurring in Central America: 'perhaps, over the years we should have intervened less, or intervened more, or intervened differently. But all these are questions of what might have been. What confronts us now is the question of what it might become.' The US destruction of the democratic Arbenz government in Guatemala in 1954, the multiple invasions of Nicaragua, the invasion of the Dominican Republic in 1965 – these and other US actions figure hardly at all in the Kissinger vision. His own devotion to the cause of Latin American democracy was, of course, well proven in the efforts he made to undermine the elected government of Chile between 1970 and 1973.

Reaganomics and the Third World

Documents such as Kissinger's served to formulate a new, measured, support for intervention. At the same time, these military strategies of the Reagan Doctrine were linked to economic mechanisms. In both cases there was a forceful use of US state power to promote favourable developments in the third world, a rejection of previous commitments to international law and international institutions, and a promotion of anti-statist 'free' forces in the market. In both cases too, the loud proclamation of new policies and solutions was accompanied by widespread social deterioration, and actual death from economic hardship, in the parts of the third world most grievously affected. But perhaps the most significant similarity between the two dimensions of

US policy was the political project underlying them, namely the reimposition of US influence on third world countries as a whole, what some writers have termed the 'recolonization' of the third world. US economic power, as much as or even more than its military power, gave it the capacity to exert forms of control on third world societies and states and to impose its wishes on them, whether directly and bilaterally, or through influence on the policies of multilateral agencies. Each policy also served to distract attention from the more negative aspects of the other. If economic policies diminished attention to the human cost of the new security and intervention policies, the rhetoric about support for freedom fighters distracted attention from the more insoluble and menacing issues of third world debt and the implications of this for the US banking system. Mexico's debts posed a far more serious threat to the USA than the reforms of Nicaragua's FSLN: but it was easier to focus attention upon the latter and so present an appearance of practicality and effectiveness. In the third world, Reaganomics was therefore a partner of, rather than an alternative to the Reagan Doctrine.

In macroeconomic policy the Administration pursued a unilateral policy towards the third world as well as towards western Europe.[4] There was little respect for considerations of 'interdependence', and for what this concept entailed – multilateral negotiations, attempts to build up 'régimes' binding states together.[5] Thus even the formal acknowledgement made by Carter to the third world's call for a New International Economic Order, first enunciated at the UN in 1974, was abandoned and forgotten. US officials said straightforwardly that they were not interested in it, and the Cancun conference of October 1981, called by the UN to promote global negotiations on the NIEO, came to nothing. Similarly, the Reagan Administration pulled out of the protracted and almost completed negotiations of the UN Conference on the Law of the Sea, rejecting state agreements on this issue: later, in the Gulf of Sirte off Libya, Reagan was to demonstrate his own view of maritime law.

The pullout from UNESCO and the harrassment of other UN agencies fitted this pattern of rejecting the multilateral dimension of relations with other states. While the annual institution of economic summits of the seven major industrialized countries was strengthened, this served to enforce the other six's acceptance of US macroeconomic policies, not to involve the USA in new interdependent patterns. The net result was clear enough: while the US economy enjoyed a boom thanks to tighter monetary and looser fiscal policy, Reagan's economic policies intensified the crisis in the third world. Interest rates rose and until the fall of the dollar in late 1987 the debts of third world countries, indexed in dollars, increased further because of that currency's appreciation. The overall economic indicators of the third world during the 1980s told their own tale. Third world GDP as a whole rose by only 1.4% per year in the period 1981–5, compared to 4.9% in the years 1976–80. The number of those living below minimum subsistence levels ran at around 800 million in the mid-1980s. While many factors contributed to this, the neglect and self-serving unilateralism of the world's strongest economy contributed mightily.

Table One

Authorised Expenditures, 1980–1988
(in US $ Millions)

	International Development and Humanitarian Assistance	International Security Assistance
1980	5,264	5,066
1981	4,420	5,068
1982	4,474	6,863
1983	4,711	8,142
1984	5,069	8,943
1985	6,496	13,730
1986	4,760	9,543
1987	4,777	9,320
1988 (est)	5,185	9,352
1989 (est)	4,890	9,486
1999 (est)	4,964	9,582

Source: Executive Office of the President, Office of Management and Budget, *Historical Tables, Budget of the US Government*, Fiscal Year, 1988

The new tone of US policy was particularly evident in attitudes to aid. US economic aid to the third world was already low, by comparison with other OECD countries. In 1983 it stood at 0.24% of GNP, compared to an OECD average of 0.36%, and figures of 0.45% for Canada, 0.74% for France, and 0.91% for

Holland. Reagan's aid policy rested on what were called the 'four pillars', guidelines that oriented the programmes of USAID and US policy in multilateral agencies, such as the UN and the World Bank. These were institution-building, technology transfer, 'policy dialogue', and support for the private sector. The latter two were particularly controversial, since they in effect involved the US government in direct attempts to alter the social policies of third world governments. The US decision to reduce the lending activities of the International Development Association, a subsidiary of the World Bank committed to lending at preferential rates to the world's poorest thirty one countries, was another part of this policy, as was the philistine assault on UNESCO. Yet perhaps the greatest change in US aid policy was the overall shift in its profile, from economic to security aid. In the 1980s annual US development aid rose by less than one third even in the best years, while security aid rose by 50% or more. The major recipients of US military aid were Israel, Egypt, Turkey, Pakistan and Greece, with enhanced allocation to El Salvador, Guatemala and Honduras. Backing for the police and military in

Table Two

US exports of major weapons to the Third World, 1976–1986.
(Figures based on SIPRI trend indicator values in US $m.,
at constant (1985) prices).

Rank Order	1976–80 Country	Share %	1981–86 Country	Share %
1	Iran	28	Egypt	23
2	Israel	15	Saudi Arabia	18
3	Saudi Arabia	9	Israel	13
4	S. Korea	9	Taiwan	7
5	Jordan	6	Pakistan	5
6	Taiwan	5	S. Korea	4
7	Egypt	3	Jordan	3
8	Morocco	3	Venezuela	2
9	Thailand	3	Thailand	2
10	Kuwait	2	Morocco/UAE	2
Total of 10		87%		78%

Source: Michael Brzoska and Thomas Ohlson, *Arms Transfers to the Third World, 1979–85*, SIPRI/OUP, 1987, p.48.

the third world constituted perhaps the fifth, and central, pillar of the new US aid programme. It formed a fitting adjunct to the overtly interventionist military and political complex that made up the Reagan Doctrine.

In the second Reagan administration, US economic policy towards the third world was slightly modified, through the policies pursued at the Department of the Treasury by James Baker. Baker, later to be first secretary of state in the Bush administration, came to the Treasury from the White House in February 1985 and proceeded to advocate more co-operative and 'internationalist' policies in US economic affairs: he collaborated to a greater degree on monetary policy with the other OECD states, and, faced with the rising crisis of third world debt and its possibly explosive impact on the US banks, he introduced measures to lessen the burden of indebtedness on Latin American and other countries. He encouraged the IMF and the World Bank to ease pressure on third world states, and launched the 'Baker Plan', under which third world debts would be alleviated by the commercial banks converting these debts into long-term bonds, thereby removing the need for the debtor states to repay on existing punitive schedules. The psychological impact of Baker's espousal of 'interdependence' was considerable: in practice, very little had changed. US economic aid to third world states did not increase, and the commercial banks declined to take up the invitation contained in the 'Baker Plan'.

The Reagan Doctrine: Five Components

By 1984 it must have been evident that the 'containment' policy of the first Reagan term based on the 'strategic' approach was not succeeding: the USA was not able to 'go to the source' in the way Haig and others had originally envisaged; the USSR was not willing to abandon third world allies as part of a diplomatic package; and the Israeli and South African campaigns had created as many problems as they had set out to solve. The US defeat in Lebanon in 1983–4 prompted Shultz above all to focus on the need for a protracted and committed use of force against hostile forces. Shultz came to see the October 1983 killing of 230 US marines in Beirut as a 1980s version of Pearl Harbour.

The impasse in Central America necessitated greater activity by the USA if it was to maintain its credibility. At the same time, the Democratic Party in Congress swung behind indirect intervention. It was through such a bipartisan 'learning process' that the Reagan Doctrine of 1985–1988 was assisted to birth.

Flanked as it was by an assertive economic unilateralism, and placed within the broader context of intensified east-west confrontation, the Reagan Doctrine itself was a policy designed to deal with third world revolutions – to prevent them, to weaken and 'bleed' them if they had already occurred, or, if possible, to overthrow them. With a felt need in Washington to respond to the revolutions of the 1970s without immediately sending in the marines, the Reagan Doctrine was, in effect, a policy of counter-revolution on the cheap. It was cheap for the USA – in terms of casualties avoided, and in terms of the contained diplomatic response of the USSR, of the more independent third world states and of opinion in other OECD countries. Within this strategic space, it had five distinct components: the first was a new theory of war, under the rubric Low Intensity Conflict; the second was that of 'pro-insurgency', of promoting military and other covert opposition to third world revolutionary régimes; the third was that of intervening in revolutionary situations to deflect revolutionary upheavals and save as much as possible of the existing régimes; the fourth was the pursuit of an 'anti-terrorist' campaign; the fifth was the ultimate, reserve, power of direct US intervention itself, against revolutions that appeared imminent or which, after their having occurred, remained vulnerable.

(i) *Low Intensity Conflict*

In US military strategy of the 1980s conflicts were divided into three categories: high, meaning nuclear war; medium, meaning conventional and regional inter-state wars; and low or irregular. Low Intensity Conflict, or LIC, became the leading military element in the Reagan Doctrine. Officially announced first in 1981, and later formulated in a number of official and semi-official documents, it had at first to compete with the 'strategic' view of third world conflict; but it came of age in 1986 with a major conference at the National Defense College in Washington addressed by George Shultz, and its full incorporation into official orthodoxy. LIC was the updated approach to irregular military activities in the third world. It drew upon US counter-insurgency thinking of the 1960s and, usually without attribution, upon the parallel British concept of Low Intensity Operations. Some of its proponents saw it as the answer to revolutionary guerrilla strategies, a kinds of 'American Leninism'. Its proponents argued that it covered up to six main kinds of operation: counter-insurgency, or the defeat of challenges to allied governments; 'pro-insurgency', or assistance to anti-communist insurgents, in effect support for the overthrow of Soviet allies; anti- and counter-terrorist activities; anti-drug policies; short-term military operations; and peace-keeping actions. It did, therefore, appear to provide a comprehensive practical and conceptual guide for waging counter-revolution in the third world of the 1980s.

The proponents of LIC stressed again and again the vague and complex character of this operation. It was 'neither simple nor short-term' wrote two leading army experts, Morelli and Ferguson. Secretary of State Shultz had stressed its 'ambiguity': 'Ambiguous warfare has exposed a chink in our armor', stated Shultz in his January 1986 address to the National Defense University.[6] To reply effectively to this 'ambiguity', and to justify and orientate US actions, the theory of LIC presented a number of distinct arguments:

(a) *the combination of military and non-military forms of combat*: the US had to be prepared to fight not just on the military front, but also using political, economic, cultural and social instruments. Prominent amongst these were Civil Action Programmes, Psychological Operations, and propaganda campaigns of a broad political character.

(b) *the need to be prepared for protracted commitments*: one of the most galling lessons of the Vietnam War was the realization that the US did not have the stamina to sustain the commitment of combat forces. Time and again LIC theorists stressed the need for the USA to have the patience, endurance, and staying power needed; thus Shultz:

> We must avoid no-win situations, but we must also have the stomach to confront the harder-to-win situations that call for prudent involvement, even when the results are slow in coming. Steadfastness and endurance are the keys to success;

71

our adversaries notice when we are impatient, uncomfortable, or vacillating. Thus, we lose our leverage, and we *make* the problem more prolonged and more difficult to resolve. Unfortunately, in the wake of Vietnam our endurance against any kind of challenge has been open to question.

(c) *minimization of US combat involvement*: while implementation of LIC certainly involved direct US military activity, this was above all in the form of assistance to indigenous forces, of government or opposition, and of small Special Operations Forces and covert operatives. LIC theorists insisted that US combat forces should not be involved in long-run, Vietnam-style operations. The 'lesson' drawn here from Vietnam was that the US effort failed because it was too direct and too large. Thus Morelli and Ferguson: 'The Army's capability to deal with low-intensity conflict is constrained at the outset – and it should be . . . if we must commit US forces to combat in a low-intensity situation, we have lost the strategic initiative. This may exacerbate the effects of change and risk the escalation of the conflict without necessarily affecting its cause'.[7] The important point about this argument is that it opposed direct US involvement not because such a deployment was seen as being inappropriate to the problem on the ground. It was a long-run, essential feature of LIC, not a second-best solution imposed from within the US political system.

(d) *the mobilization of support within the USA*: the political and psychological components of LIC were related not just to combat inside the country to be 'saved from communism' (point a) but also to the situation within the USA itself. Another of the 'lessons' of Vietnam was that the war was lost as much within the USA as in Vietnam itself. The answer was clear enough: great effort had to be put into 'public diplomacy', mobilizing and maintaining a domestic constituency – within the US government, in Congress, in the media, and in the public sphere as a whole. It was on this front that Reagan himself played such a central role, posturing and lying at endless conferences and TV addresses in order to spread anxiety about Central America. The passage of bills granting aid to the *contras* epitomized the way in which this vital domestic operation was carried out. The privatization of support for the *contras*, through the activity of Political Action

Committees and right-wing pressure groups, and through Oliver North's gunrunning enterprises, had a political as well as a financial role: its primary aim was to augment the funds flowing to the *contras* and circumvent Congress, but it also served to increase the degree of political commitment, participation and sense of importance felt by right-wing activists on Central American issues, and to curb the influence of critics at home. It was Oliver North himself who spelt this out most clearly when testifying before Congress: the Vietnam War was lost, he said, not in Indo-China, but in 'this city'.

The theory of LIC had an ambiguous character. It was an attempt to implement a new counter-revolutionary policy in the third world, but it appeared to involve a tacit recognition of the limits of American power. The conservative revival in the USA in the late 1970s was accompanied by a widespread emphasis upon the need to use force in the third world, and to overcome the effects of the 'Vietnam Syndrome'. Reagan pledged himself to build up American power, in the counter-revolutionary as much as in the strategic nuclear fields. In 1980–1 there was talk of action against Cuba, direct US military involvements elsewhere in the third world, and of the 'curing' of America of the Vietnam Syndrome. One of the most influential analyses of the Vietnam War, Harry Summers' *On Strategy*, argued in the best Clausewitzian manner that the US mistake in Vietnam was in *not* seeing it as a conventional war with North Vietnam, and acting accordingly. However, US public opinion, while certainly easily aroused about such matters as 'terrorism' and Soviet influence, did not swing away from its anti-interventionist stand. Reagan found it politically prohibitive to engage in a direct assault on his *betes noires* in Central America. Overall, throughout the eight years of Reagan's presidency the direct reassertion of US military power in the third world was neither as domestically popular, as extensive or as successful, as might initially have been expected in 1979.

LIC can be seen as a recognition of these limits – an attempt to circumvent the limitations on American power while pursuing the counter-revolutionary goals that Reagan had long and consistently maintained, and eroding domestic resistance to such interventions.[8] There is, however, another way of analysing the theory of Low Intensity Conflict and the broader themes of the

Doctrine. This is not as a second-best, a substitute for the most desirable but impractical policy – direct military intervention in the traditional sense – but rather as the most appropriate means of dealing with the kind of challenge posed by political and social explosions in the third world. Seen in this light, the lesson of Vietnam was not that more firepower would have carried the day, but rather that the resort to direct intervention, from 1965 to 1973, was mistaken from the start, and could not have attained victory even if it had been carried out with greater numbers of troops and more political determination. This is an important component of the LIC analysis of Vietnam, the main alternative to the Summers approach. The political problem posed within the USA was, in these terms, not that of gradually winning support for the invasion of another country, but rather of consolidating long-run support – in Congress, among the public, the military and the government – for LIC involvements. The emphasis placed by proponents of LIC upon the need for patience, endurance, stamina and so forth indicated that this was the direction in which at least some leading strategists were moving. Kissinger in his 1984 *Report*, and Shultz in his January 1986 speech, spelt this out clearly.

(ii)   *Pro-insurgency: A new form of covert action*

The classic variant of 'covert action' by the CIA was that of clandestine support for military coups against revolutionary of reforming régimes. This was the form that secret action against left-wing régimes took in the 1950s, 1960s and in the 1974–1980 period and it ranked up a significant number of successes: Syria 1949, Iran 1953, Guatemala 1954, Congo 1961, Brazil 1964, Chile 1973.[9] In none of these was CIA action the *sole* factor in guaranteeing the counter-revolutionary outcome, but in all of them US support, diplomatic in public, financial and organizational in secret, was a major input into the whole process. This form of covert action rested, however, on one essential prerequisite: the relative vulnerability of the armed forces in the target country to such subversion. In other words, it was only possible when the revolutionary or nationalist government had not been able to transform the state machine, and the military in particular. Often, as in Iran and Chile, the régime was trying to avoid a confrontation with the military and so treated it with special forebearance, even as pro-government officers in the armed forces were being assassinated by the right (General Afshar Tus in Iran, the police chief murdered in 1952 by British agents; General René Schneider in Chile, assassinated in 1970). When the CIA went into action against the revolutions of the 1970s this option was not available, precisely because the revolutionaries had destroyed the old state machine, including its army, and replaced it with their own revolutionary armed forces. As in the case of Cuba during the period 1959–1961, the CIA was thrown back on a surrogate form of covert action – aid to right-wing guerrillas.

The promotion of guerrilla warfare against revolutionary régimes is as old as counter-revolution itself.[10] The very term 'guerrilla' or 'little war' was first used to describe the British-backed harassment of Napoleon's forces in Spain by Spanish counter-revolutionaries in the 1800s. Much of the Allied support for the anti-Bolshevik White Armies in the period 1918–20 took the form of arms deals with Czarist *contras*. In the post-1945 period there have been several attempts to weaken or overthrow revolutionary régimes through the use of guerrillas – the British and Americans sent hundreds of right-wing exiles into Albania in the late 1940s in a fruitless campaign against Enver Hoxha's régime; the CIA for a number of years armed and trained exiled Tibetans for action against the Chinese army in their country. During the Indo-Chinese wars, the CIA and the US Special Forces used irregular armies, in Vietnam the Montagnards and Nung, in Laos the Meo, to harrass and divert the communist forces. In 1975 aid flowed to UNITA in Angola, while weapons began to reach the Afghan *mujahidin* in 1980.

However, with the advent of the Reagan Administration, support for right-wing guerrillas, what was now termed 'pro-insurgency', acquired a new and special prominence, and the expenditure and effort devoted to promoting such conflicts greatly increased. Backing for 'freedom fighters' became one central part of the new LIC policy and was linked to an overall offensive strategy against the Soviet alliance system in the third world. Under the direction of William C. Casey, who ran the CIA from 1981 to 1986, the Agency placed itself at the centre of these counter-revolutionary operations: they were reportedly directed by a committee that met in Room 208 of the Old Executive Building across the road from the White House. The '208 Committee' included representatives of the CIA, the National Security Council, the Department of Defense, and the Department of State, and its decisions were ratified by the National Security Planning Group, which included the president and key national security advisers.[11] A complex network of executive bodies was set up to administer this process as was later to become clear from the Iran-Contra revelations. In the aftermath of Irangate, and Casey's resignation and death, the 208 Committee was dissolved: instead, in early 1987, a new 'Board of Low Intensity Conflict' was set up within the National Security Council and in June 1987 Reagan signed an authorization for a new comprehensive LIC policy.

The CIA provided support for at least four counter-revolutionary guerrilla movements in the third world from 1981 to 1988: those in Cambodia, Afghanistan, Angola and Nicaragua. The USA had been involved in the first three prior to 1981,

Publicly reported US aid to guerrilla movements, FY86 and FY87

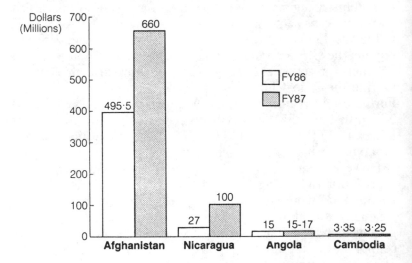

Source: Raymond Copson *The Reagan Doctrine: US Assistance to Anti-Marxist Guerrillas,* Congressional Research Service, Issue Brief, March 1988
Note: Data on covert programs is taken from reports appearing in the press.

but the scale and degree of commitment increased greatly after Reagan entered the White House. In financial terms, by far the largest operation was Afghanistan, which in 1986 alone received an estimated $470 million, $630 million in 1987 and over $2 billion in the period as a whole. It was only in that country that US support was going directly to a force that was killing Russians: official Soviet figures listed 13,000 killed up to May 1988. Of the four campaigns, two of them had internal roots within the country – Afghanistan and Angola – and were, in addition, supported by neighbouring anti-communist states, by Pakistan and South Africa respectively. The Cambodian and Nicaraguan forces were remnants of defeated régimes which had a peripheral existence on the frontiers of the states concerned and would not have survived, or, in the case of the *contras* come into existence, had the CIA not supported them. The CIA may also have been involved in other right-wing guerrilla movements, such as Ronnie Brunswijke's National Surinamese Liberation Army, which in July 1986 began operation in the east of that country. Aid to Brunswijke came via Surinam's neighbour to the east – French Guyana, which sent aid across the Marowijne river, and acted as a conduit for aid coming from Holland. France had worked closely with the CIA in Chad, and may well have done so in Surinam too: France had its own reasons for being hostile to Surinam, namely the close relations between that country and France's opponents in Chad, Libya.

The motivation behind this pro-insurgency policy was, at first sight, evident enough: to assist in the overthrow of régimes the USA disliked, and to curb Soviet power at the margins. Yet, on closer examination, the LIC-Contra policy was not so coherent. First, while in Afghanistan the guerrillas did place the Soviet forces under great strain, in three of the four main cases there was little likelihood of the guerrillas succeeding in ousting the incumbent régime. The guerrillas of Cambodia, Angola and Nicaragua could roam around much of the country and cause great damage, but they could not replace the incumbent power. Second, US support was not given to *all* groups championing the cause of anti-communism in the third world. Thus the MNR (or RENAMO) in Mozambique, established and backed by South Africa, was not aided by the USA, despite lobbying in MNR's favour by right-wing senators. Indeed Washington provided some backing to the Mozambiquan government ($85 million in economic and food aid in 1987) and when Reagan met President Chissano in October 1987 he promised to continue this aid. Despite Reagan Administration hostility to the Ethiopian government, and its maintenance of an economic blockade on the country (for all transactions except emergency food supplies), appeals for aid from the right-wing Ethiopian People's Democratic Alliance in 1982 – for a six-month grant of $547,000 to train 350 guerrillas cadres – were refused. No significant aid was provided to the substantial guerrilla movements operating against the Ethiopian government in Eritrea and Tigre, which were, in any case, under Marxist leadership. There were reports in 1986 of new funds going to Ethiopian opposition forces, but these seemed to be of little more than of nuisance value. The fate of the once-prized anti-communist Chinese forces based in Taiwan hardly needs mentioning. Third, the degree of ideological inconsistency involved in some of these support campaigns was striking, even for the bizarre world of covert operations. Thus in Cambodia, food aid and at least indirect military aid was going to the Khmers Rouges, the ferociously anti-American communists who had ruled Cambodia from 1975 until 1979. In Afghanistan, the social programme of the *mujahidin* was little different, and hardly more accommodating, than that of their western neighbour Khomeini.

This incoherence prompted the question of what the goals of such covert operations were, of why the USA promoted forces that, Afghanistan excepted, stood no apparent chance of success. A number of distinct reasons for this LIC policy seemed to be operating in a simultaneous and overlapping manner. Such policies did not, however, need to be coherent: they could pursue various goals simultaneously. First, there was the desire to impose as high a cost as possible on the USSR and its allies, while the USA was not directly involved in the conflicts. The loss of life, the diversion of financial and administrative resources, the political strains provoked by LIC wars – all these were welcome to an anti-communist crusading administration. They helped to tie down the USSR and its allies; in the idiom of the Reagan Administration, to 'bleed' them. Secondly, there was the desire to appeal to US domestic opinion. Reagan's speeches about 'freedom fighters' and their ideals formed part of the overall mobilization of US domestic opinion behind his policies. The less results his policy had on the ground, the more he needed to be seen to be doing something. Thirdly, there was the desire for revenge. A policy-making elite that had endured of Vietnam, Angola and other 'defeats' was now enjoying the novel sensation of having their own guerrillas to use against revolutionaries. In a characteristic speech in January 1985 William Casey boasted of the shift of initiative in world affairs: 'Whereas in the 1960s and 1970s anti-western causes attracted recruits throughout the third world, this decade has emerged as the decade of freedom fighters resisting communist régimes'.[12]

There were two other, often-cited reasons for the pro-insurgency component of LIC which placed these individual problems in a broader strategic context. One was that of harrassing revolutionary régimes in order to prevent them from encouraging revolutionary forces in other states. Thus Nicaragua was presented as threatening El Salvador and other Latin American states, Angola as menacing Namibia, and Cambodia and its Vietnamese allies as menacing Thailand. LIC was therefore presented as part of a regional diplomatic and deterrent strategy. On a broader scale, the US role in these conflicts was seen as part of the overall process of bargaining and competing with the USSR. In a revived form, this was the old policy of 'linkage', with the USA suggesting that if the USSR made concessions on regional conflicts, by allowing US-backed forces into the régimes, then the USA would be more accommodating on arms talks. In the early months of the Reagan Administration, and again in the weeks preceding the November 1985 Geneva Summit, this issue was presented as central to US foreign policy. Reagan's speech to the UN in September 1985 listed Soviet actions in five countries as underlying the loss of life and continuation of conflict. The five were: Angola, Nicaragua, Cambodia, Afghanistan and Ethiopia. He called for Soviet 'disengagement' and US-Soviet negotiations on these regional crises.

This 'bargaining' approach to LIC conflicts was, in either version, misleading. As far as the 'domino' effects of third world revolutions are concerned, it was not the actions of established revolutionary régimes but the example of their success in the first place that threatened to have knock-on consequences.

Even when Nicaragua stopped providing aid to the FMLN in El Salvador in 1981, US backing for the *contras* increased. The argument that the USA was arming the *contras* to interdict supplies to El Salvador was a deception. The global argument had equally little foundation, for a different reason: the USSR was not prepared to deal in this way. In the midst of World War II, a somewhat inebriated Stalin and Churchill negotiated late at night, on the back of an envelope, about spheres of influence in Europe: but no such agreement was possible with the USSR of the 1980s. While the Russians were willing to discuss regional differences, and had been keen to do so during the early 1980s when Washington was not, they rejected any kind of explicit bargain of the kind that CIA support for guerrillas was supposed to facilitate. Nicaragua was not to be traded for Afghanistan. Pro-insurgency's other goals, those involving the weakening of third world states, were more attainable.

(iii)   *Finessing revolutionary crises*

The policy of Low Intensity Conflict and covert action was directed against revolutionary régimes that had already established themselves, and which now provided targets for sabotage and harrassment. Of equal importance was the task of preventing further revolutions from occurring, of ensuring that the stalled wave of 1974–80 did not continue. Reagan's 1984 boast that no revolutions had occurred during his presidency was accurate, and reflected the effort put into this endeavour by his officials. To do so without deploying US forces, the administration relied on two main policies: first, 'security assistance', enhanced support of military counter-insurgency campaigns; second, political intervention in situations of revolutionary crisis.

We have seen how 'security assistance' grew substantially in the Reagan years. Support for third world counter-insurgency had been the mainstay of US policy in the early 1960s and had notched up many successes – especially in Latin America. The death of Che Guevara in Bolivia in 1967 marked the zenith of its success, but it was soon obscured by the protracted defeat of Vietnam. Under the Carter Administration 'security' assistance was downplayed and aid to a number of states, including Somoza's Nicaragua and Guatemala, terminated. Reagan moved decisively to reverse this trend. The overall increase in 'security' aid to third world states reflected this shift as did institutional changes in Washington itself: the establishment of the US Army 1st Special Operations Command, SOCOM, and the Joint Special Operations Agency, JSOA, within the Joint Chiefs of Staff were part of this new counter-insurgency activism. Old practices and personnel from the wars of Indo-China returned.

Two well-publicized cases of this kind of activity were Chad and El Salvador. In the former, technical and military aid were provided to the forces of Hissene Habre, who was fighting Libyan-backed forces in the north of his country. The Chad maneouvres, in 1981 and 1982, were carried out with the assistance of friendly intelligence forces, from France, Egypt and Sudan. Chad represented the CIA's outstanding success during the first Reagan Administration. In El Salvador, a large-scale counter-insurgency operation was underway, with the USA providing arms, advisers and intelligence support for the régime. While the official number of US advisers was kept low, at fifty-five, in order to deflect Congressional criticism, thousands of US military personnel were involved in this operation, in El Salvador itself and in backup roles in Honduras, from where intelligence and combat planes flew in support of counter-insurgency activities. Between 1980 and 1987 US aid to El Salvador totalled nearly $1 billion, and the armed forces were expanded from 12,000 to over 53,000 in the same period.

Of equal importance in preventing revolutionary triumphs was the parallel political strategy of confiscating and deflecting revolts before they succeeded. The defeat in Iran had provoked a wide-ranging policy debate in Washington about how the USA could have prevented Khomeini from coming to power. While opinions differed on many aspects of this saga, one common goal emerged: that the USA should have been able to save the régime (above all, the army), while removing the Shah. The problem with Iran was not just that the Shah fled, but that the whole régime crumbled with him. The lesson was that such situations should be managed so that the hated dictator could leave, but that the régime he headed would remain. Ideally, of course, figures from his own régime would change sides at the last moment and present themselves as champions of an alternative régime, thus guaranteeing continuity of the state and appropriating some of the opposition's credit. Similarly, the USA could support the régime until the very end, yet endorse such a transition and come up smelling of roses. A parallel 'lesson' was drawn by right-wing analysts of Nicaragua: Carter should have forced Somoza out in 1978, installed a 'sanitized' National Guard régime, and so blocked the revolution of 1979.[13]

No other component of Reagan's foreign policy caused so much surprise as this manipulation of revolution. In no less than five countries the USA participated in transition processes that implemented the lessons of Iran and Nicaragua. The state remained: the dictator departed. In Sudan, El Salvador, Haiti, the Philippines and South Korea the USA was able to do what it could not do in Iran. In Sudan widespread popular unrest in April 1985 led to military action against President al-Nimeiry: he went into exile in Egypt and his former lieutenants in the army assumed power. The elected government of Sadiq al-Mahdi was virtually paralysed from the start. In El Salvador, the right-wing strongman Roberto d'Aubuisson, elected head of the National Assembly in 1982, was kept out of power by US pressure and displaced in the 1984 presidential elections by José Napoleón Duarte. The El Salvadoran armed forces were not significantly affected by this procedure, which gave to the régime a new, more appealing image. As a result the counter-insurgency war was prosecuted all the more vigourously. By 1988, with Duarte dying of cancer and the death squads once more unleashed, ARENA, the right-wing party founded by d'Aubuisson in 1981, was acting as though it were already in power. In Haiti, a replay of the Sudanese scenario occurred, and in February 1986, 'Baby Doc' Duvalier and his associates fled the country, leaving behind the régime headed by General Namphy and other associates of the Duvalier family, including the vigilante *Tontons Macoutes*. The danger of 'Cuban' influence, so feared by US officials in the event of continued Duvalierite rule, was removed, for the time being, and demands for a thorough purge of the state, for *démacoutisation*, were resisted. In November 1987 military units killed opposition supporters in a campaign to block free elections, and in June 1988 Namphy ousted elected President Manigat before himself falling to a coup on 17 September. In the Philippines, Ferdinand Marcos was ousted after army officers long loyal to him staged an operatic revolt in Manila and declared support for Corazón Aquino, the victorious opposition candidate in the 6 February elections. The armed forces remained, however, intact and by 1988 Mrs Aquino appeared more and more their hostage.

In the ROK, or South Korea, the military dictatorship of Chun Doo Hwan – in power since 1980 – was facing continued pressure from student demonstrators, religious leaders, human rights activists, and political exiles with a following in the USA. Chun had replaced the assassinated dictator Park Jung-Hee and held power through the military, using a manipulated electoral college to validate his tenure. By mid-1987 pressure for change had grown to the point where Chun was forced to concede that free elections should be held: these were convened in July 1987, with the result that two opposition candidates, Kim Dae Jung and Kim Young Sam divided the opposition vote (51% in total), and a representative of the ruling party, Roh Tae Woo, was elected as president (with 35% of the vote). Chun himself was therefore removed from power, and he and his associates were later subject to public criticism and prosecution for their conduct in office: but the management of the transition, and the division within the opposition, enabled the régime itself, a direct continuation of the military dictatorship installed by the USA before the Korean war, to survive. The ruling Democratic Justice Party was a tool of the armed forces. The new President Roh Tae Woo was a former general, who had helped Chun come to power in 1980; his power rested, as had Chun's, on the armed forces; and seven of the ministers in his first cabinet were inherited from the outgoing one.

In all five of these transitions, there was a significant US diplomatic input. The USA was not the main cause of the changes, as was sometimes stated by US officials claiming 'credit' for the ending of these tyrannies. But there was certainly a US contribution in guiding the transitions, once they had begun, towards more acceptable outcomes. In the Sudanese case, US officials encouraged Nimeiry not to try and return to Sudan when the crisis erupted during a visit he was making to Washington, and they encouraged Egypt to give him asylum: the new Sudanese rulers knew they had US backing for their action. In El Salvador, it was direct US pressure that kept d'Aubuisson from assuming the presidency and which led in 1983 to the 'cleaning up' of the El Salvadoran army and the reduction, until 1987–8, in overt death squad activity. In Haiti, US officials had long urged Duvalier to go, and it was a US plane that took the dictator and his family out of the country. In the Philippines, US policy began to change in late 1984 with a decision to promote 'political reform' and in November 1985 Marcos yielded to the USA in promising the elections that were to bring about his downfall. The CIA-backed *Radio Veritas* openly supported the revolt of the military leaders Enrile and Ramos that brought Marcos down and US officials had previously urged the army to revolt if Marcos tried to falsify the election results; it was US officials who took Marcos out of the country and prevented him from returning to his stronghold in the Ilocos region of northern Luzon. In Korea, the USA had backed Chun through 1986, but with the shift in popular attitudes, Washington began in 1987 to encourage a pre-emptive transition. On 6 February 1987 Assistant Secretary of State for East Asian and Pacific Affairs, Gaston Sigur, called for 'a more open and legitimate political system' in the ROK, and, after several attempts by Chun to ensure his survival, Reagan himself wrote to him on 17 June urging political reform. In order to pre-empt a dissolution of the state, US officials also worked, as in the Philippines and El Salvador, to win army officers over to a transition policy.

The role of the USA in these changes was essentially twofold. The first was the partial or complete withdrawal of support from a régime that had hitherto relied on US backing: since part of any revolution is the weakening of the established régime, the withdrawal of US support, expressed through a cutting of aid or an expression of disapproval, constituted a vital part of the shift within these countries. The second element was the diplomatic guiding of the crisis itself, to ensure a speedy departure or neutralization of the unwanted candidate and clear backing for the new leadership. This policy had failed in Iran, because the Khomeini opposition was strong enough to prevent the USA from installing a post-Shah régime under Shahpur Bakhtiar. It failed too in Nicaragua in 1978–9, because no blocking alternative could be produced, as it had failed in Cuba, with Batista, in 1958. In Sudan and El Salvador the results of revolt were ephemeral. Haiti, the Philippines and Korea were more successful. The changes effected had the negative consequences of unleashing popular protests and allowing greater open debate, but this was a price worth paying in that it save the state machine; it enabled a pro-Western successor régime to claim credit for itself and to buy time for restabilization. Many of those who had played a role in undermining the old régime – the communists and southern guerrillas in the Sudan, the FMLN in El Salvador, the urban protesters in Haiti, the NPA in the Philippines, the student opposition in the ROK – were thereby excluded from power.

(iv) *'Anti-terrorism' and 'Counter-terrorism'*

The question of 'terrorism', an issue current in political conflict for many decades, became a subject of special concern and indignation in the 1980s. According to the conventional wisdom, western states were now subject to a vicious assault by third world extremists, assisted by hostile states such as the USSR, Cuba, North Korea and Libya. The 'terrorist' became the demon of the age, and the fight against terrorism a central part of Ronald Reagan's crusade. This fight had two components: 'anti-terrorism', or measures designed to prevent terrorist attacks, and 'counter-terrorism', the use of terror against those believed to be responsible for, or contemplating, such actions.[14]

In this, as in other matters, it is rather important to separate the sense from the nonsense. Certain kinds of violent action had indeed become more common in 1970s and 1980s, and had claimed innocent victims – in hijackings, random bomb explosions and kidnappings. Those who carried out such actions – in Ireland, the Basque country, Palestine, the Punjab or wherever – bore a significant responsibility for the reaction their pernicious activities provoked. They did nothing to advance the liberation of the peoples they claimed to be fighting for, and did much to discredit and isolate them, as well as to embolden their enemies. But the manner in which the issue of terrorism was presented in the West was itself confused and self-serving. First, the great majority of acts of terror committed in the world, in the 1980s and long before, were committed not by freebooters and dissidents, but by states, against their own subjects. The violence of revolutionaries paled before the brutality of those opposed to change. South Africa and Israel, to name two obvious examples of countries said to be victims of 'terrorism', killed many more of their opponents in terror raids, outside their frontiers and within, than either the ANC or the PLO. Second, even if the criterion of political terror was that it should be committed by actors other than states, the great majority of its victims were not the diplomats, travellers and shoppers of the richer states, or the privileged inhabitants of Tel Aviv and Johannesburg, but the poor of the third world themselves. Most Arab terror was visited on other Arabs, most Iranian against Iranians. In Sri Lanka, the Punjab and the Philippines the same applied. The hysteria over 'terror', manipulated and enhanced in the 1980s, was a fabrication designed to serve political ends.

Of all the issues which gave a new flavour to US foreign policy under Reagan, this was the most pungent. This had been an issue in US political discourse since the late 1960s, and had initially been directed at Palestinian groups who hijacked planes and provoked civilian casualties in Israel. The term 'terrorist' was then expanded, to cover all those using military means for undesirable political purposes. The distinction between those who were fighting for national independence or social justice in a controlled manner and those who used indiscriminate violence was obscured. Under the Carter Administration a number of third world countries were classified as 'aiding terrorism', and various forms of economic and diplomatic sanctions imposed on them. The anxiety about terrorism reached its peak during the hostage crisis in Iran when the people holding the diplomats hostage were classed as 'terrorist'. The image of the third world crazy, preferably bearded and Islamic, was here to stay.

The campaign against terrorism fulfilled three major functions. First, it served as a means of denying legitimacy to all third world liberation and opposition groups. Second, it aroused anxiety of a special kind within the USA and served to drive home most effectively the message of an external menace. Third, it was an additional instrument with which to belabour the USSR, which stood accused of aiding terrorism, either through specific KGB links, or through a generic support for third world, especially Arab causes. The long-running saga of the supposed KGB-Bulgarian involvement in the 1981 assassination attempt on the Pope was a leitmotif of this campaign. Anti-terrorism then became an important part of the

Reagan Doctrine. On 3 April 1984 Reagan signed National Security Decision Directive 138: this authorized 'counter-terrorism', pre-emptive strikes and reprisals against 'terrorists' operating outside the USA, and allowed for improved intelligence on suspect groups, the preparation of a list of targets to be hit, and training of FBI, CIA and Special Forces squads for counter-terrorist activities. A new office for Counter-Terrorism and Emergency Planning was set up in the State Department.

If the initial and continuously important goal of the 'anti-terrorist' and 'counter-terrorist' campaigns was that of discrediting opponents of the USA, the Reagan Doctrine found new reasons for this 'great fear' and made it even more central to US policy. On the one hand, it provided the pretext for a number of direct actions by the USA against third world opponents: the air attacks against Libya in April 1986 were the most obvious example. On the other hand, it served the function of displacement – the blaming on others of what the blamer himself is doing. In the case of the USA, the most striking feature of the Reagan Doctrine was the way in which Washington itself came to be a promoter and organizer of terrorist actions. The *mujahidin* in Afghanistan, UNITA in Angola and the Nicarguan *contras* were all responsible for abominable actions in their pursuit of 'freedom' – massacring civilians, torturing and raping captives, destroying schools, hospitals and economic installations, killing and mutilating prisoners. In his eight years in the White House Reagan was responsible for the deaths of tens of thousands of people through terrorism, many times more than the PLO or other favourite targets of his righteous wrath. Certain particular cases of 'counter-terrorist' terror were given wide publicity: the CIA handbook for the *contras*, advising them on assassination, and the car bomb in Beirut that killed dozens of people in December 1983, carried out by a group aided by the CIA, were among the most striking examples. But overall, the demagogy of anti- and counter-terrorism fitted comfortably into the strategy of the Reagan Doctrine, and into the campaign to mobilize more support within the USA for these policies.

Perhaps the most curious component of the terrorism issue, and of the use to which it was put in distracting attention from underlying causes, was the concept of 'narco-terrorism' and its correlate, the 'narco-guerrilla'. This term, apparently first used in 1984, was said to identify a link between third world, specifically Latin American, revolutionaries, and the flow of narcotics into the USA. Thus Cuba, Nicaragua, and later Panama were accused of organizing this trade, flooding the US with cocaine and heroin to finance their policies. In reality, the main suppliers of Latin America drugs to the US market were gangsters and landowners, above all in Colombia, not the guerrilla movements or revolutionary states, and it was associates of the CIA, notably the Afghan *mujahidin* and Thai potentates, who provided much of the Asian supply. As for responsibility, it was, of course, the self-generated demands of the US public, coupled with the lax enforcement by state authorities, that allowed the traffic to continue. Rarely can the mechanism of displacement, transferring attention from those responsible, have been so evident.

(v) *Asserting US power*

When Reagan was elected in 1980, his opponents saw in him a return to the militarism and interventionism of earlier days. He himself talked of the need to overcome the 'Vietnam Syndrome', and it was expected that the Marines and the 82nd Airborne would be fanning out to subdue the third world, while Haig, then Secretary of State, talked of the need to 'go to the source'. In this direct form, we know that Reagan did *not* fulfil his initial menace. Where the US did use force, against Lebanon and Grenada, and twice against Libya, the actions were of little military significance, given the weakness of the target states. But if Reagan was unable to overcome the Vietnam Syndrome he was able to develop an alternative interventionist strategy, a preparation of US forces to supplement the other dimensions of counter-revolutionary strategy, and to provide an option for direct use if and when it became possible. This capacity for direct intervention was an alternative to the Reagan Doctrine in the strict sense, but provided an important reinforcement and fallback for it.

In developing this capability, the Reagan Administration pursued three broad programmes. The first was increased expenditure on military hardware that could be used for third world interventions. The logistical failures involved in the April 1980 hostage rescue mission to Iran underlined the general sense that the USA suffered from military incompetence. As a result, there was a substantial increase in intervention capabilities. First, the special operations forces – Green Berets, Delta Force and so on – were expanded, numbering 20,900 by the end of the decade, or 80% more than in 1981. Second, there was an increased investment in amphibious assault ships and special operations equipment, such as low-flying aircraft. The planned large-scale expansion in US naval forces, from 450 to over 600 major ships, was part of this enhancement.[15] Even if, by 1988, budget constraints reduced the full implementation of this buildup, it did serve substantially to enlarge US maritime power. Third, the USA expanded its base infrastructure in sensitive regions of the world. This has been particularly crucial in the region of the Persian Gulf, with new facilities in Oman, Saudi Arabia, Turkey and Kenya, and in Central America, with the massive infrastructural programme in Honduras.[16] The Reagan Doctrine was above all else concerned with these two areas. Such base programmes served two functions: to prepare the grounds for any possible future intervention, and, in the interim, to deter and intimidate rival forces. Fourth, the US army engaged in widespread manoeuvres in third world states and on the borders of hostile régimes: the recurrent Big Pine manoeuvres in Honduras, the annual Bright Star exercises in Egypt and Oman, and the Team Spirit manoeuvres in South Korea all formed part of this programme. Their purpose, apart from preparing for the eventuality of limited war intervention, was to intimidate and, as in the case of manoeuvres off the coast of Libya in March 1986, to provoke.

The use of air power in the Libyan raid of April 1986 typified another aspect of the Reagan Doctrine, and one that may lie closer to its heart than has as yet been recognized. This is that it was a theatrical policy, a demonstration of force against a stereotypically disliked third world leader, and for that reason very attractive to US leaders – the raid was virtually 'forced upon' them, to use their own rhetoric. This aspect of the use of force had, however, little to do with the problem at hand on the ground, or with the resolution of conflict: it had much more to do with internal politics of the USA, whose people, it was said, 'wanted to see something done'. Shultz and his associates had been smarting since the setbacks in Lebanon in late 1983 and the administration had painted Libya as the major source of terrorism in the region. An officially-generated sense of frustration, at the levels of both Washington and public opinion, led to the April 1986 strike.

Political constraints on using US military power had none-theless persisted and they had had one further consequence as far as planning for intervention was concerned. The need to avoid casualties amongst ground troops of the kind sustained in Vietnam led instead to an emphasis upon compensating forms of attack that obviated this possibility: long-range naval artillery bombardment and attacks from the air. In the Lebanon, it was the *New Jersey* that played the leading role in attacking Druze po-sitions in September 1983. In Libya the April 1986 strikes were carried out by the USAF. Plans for intervention in Nicaragua were believed to rely heavily upon air and naval bombardment, and in particular on air strikes on FSLN facilities in Managua, before any troops were committed.

A major locus of resistance to direct intervention was the US armed forces itself, who remembered the costs of Vietnam and wished to ensure that no such high-risk adventures are undertaken again. US military planners appeared to be happy with LIC, and many senior military officials spoke in favour of the expanded base and maneouvre policies of the 1980's; but there remained considerable anxiety at the top about direct US involvement in third world conflicts. This was evident in the wake of the Lebanon affair, and in 1984–7 provoked enormous, if unspoken, unease about what the USA would do if Khomeini's forces broke through the Iraqi ranks and seemed about to march on Saudi Arabia. It also underlay thinking on Central America, even though the logistics there were most favourable to a direct US role. These concerns apparently prompted a noticeably cautious, indeed restrictive declaration by Defense Secretary Weinberger in October 1985 on the conditions under which the USA should become involved in third world wars. Weinberger's conditions were: that the occasion be 'deemed vital to our national interest or that of our allies'; the troops should go in 'with the clear intention of winning'; there should be 'clearly defined political and military objectives'; there must be constant reassessment of the relation between objectives and forces committed; there must be Congressional support; the sending of US forces should be a 'last resort'. Weinberger stressed the need for political backing at home for any such action, and opposed a policy whereby US forces were drawn gradually into third world conflicts, such as Central America. These conditions were such as to make it almost impossible for the USA to fight any war in the third world at all. In the end, Reagan kept within the Weinberger rules: but up to the end of Reagan's presidency it was an open question whether, in the face of the Doctrine's failures, especially in Central America, this internal military resistance to direct intervention would persist.

One element of US military thinking that remained very much outside this composite Reagan Doctrine was the use of nuclear weapons. As already indicated, the attempt to re-establish the Clausewitzian links between politics and war through LIC in the third world was paralleled by the attempt to do so in the nuclear field, with SDI: both were elements of the Reagan programme that, almost unexpected by anyone in 1980–1981, had become central to the policies of the second term. But these had little connection with each other in operational terms, and nuclear weapons were not a visible part of the third world military buildup of the early 1980s, beyond some general speculation about the use of cruise missiles in third world crisis situations. The link between the two areas of military policy was, however, given striking expression in January 1988 with the publication of a Pentagon report entitled *Discriminate Deterrence*. This empha-sized the extent to which threats to the USA had, since 1945, come not from the USSR but from the less developed world, and it repeated many of the themes about US vulnerability and preparedness found in earlier discussions: the difficulties of access, by air and sea, to third world areas; the need for domestic support; the importance of using the country's techno-logical superiority; the avoidance of direct involvement. But it introduced a new element applicable to both the Soviet and third world contexts, namely that of a flexibility of nuclear response and the use of high-technology conventional weapons. Stressing above all the threat from the third world, *Discriminate Deterrence* highlighted many of the nuclear and global issues latent in the more detailed focus of the LIC and Reagan Doctrine approaches. This report was explicitly intended to forge a bi-partisan consensus on security issues to carry over into the next presidency: as such it represented the incorporation into any such future programme of the central components of the Reagan Doctrine, *plus* the option of using 'smart' nuclear weapons.

Verdicts and Explanations

The overall balance-sheet of the Reagan policy in the third world was, in the end, a mixed one. On the one hand, Reagan failed to overcome the deep-seated resistance of the US public to direct US intervention in the third world, and with the breaking of the Iran-Contra scandal in late 1986 it became evident that there was still considerable Congressional opposition to some forms of covert US intervention in the third world. By the time Bush was elected in 1988 the more energetic 'pro-insurgency' school was on the defensive as far as Central America was concerned. Casey was dead, North awaiting trial. Most of the right-wing guerrillas supported under the Reagan Doctrine failed to achieve power, and the one potential victory for the Doctrine was in Afghanistan. When Reagan left office in January 1989, the Sandinistas, the MPLA and the Heng Samrin government were still there. Yet as Afghanistan indicated, the combination of political, military and economic pressure on third world régimes could force such states into retreat and into political and foreign policy concessions that went against their initial inclinations. Two of the other surviving régimes – Nicaragua and Cambodia – were forced to negotiate with their opponents, while in Surinam, the military régime had to cede power to the civilian oppo-sition in November 1987. Moreover, the development of the Reagan Doctrine in 1985, with its intensified pressure on Soviet allies in the third world, coincided with the advent to power of the Gorbachev leadership in the USSR, and to the adoption of a more conciliatory and 'realist' approach in Moscow to third world crises. The result was that by 1987 and 1988 the USSR, intent upon economizing its commitments to its allies and on improving relations with the USA, was prepared to make substantial concessions in the third world, and to urge its embattled allies to do likewise. The Reagan Doctrine, for all its flaws, therefore contributed to a strategic shift in favour of the USA that marked Soviet-US relations from 1985 onwards.

One further long-term success of Reagan's would seem to have been that he shifted the centre of the policy debate within the USA to the right, and used his rhetoric about American values and support for 'freedom' to make a modified version of the interventionism associated with his name a necessary feature of Bush's presidency in 1989–1992. If Reagan was unable to break resistance to the direct commitment of American troops, he did make active support for guerrillas in Afghanistan something of a talisman that commanded widespread bipartisan support. In February 1988 there occurred an improbable Congressional revolt when a bipartisan initiative, a Senate vote of 77-0 spearheaded by anti-communist Christian fanatics, forced Reagan to harden his line on negotiations with Moscow over Afghanistan, by promising to continue aid to the *mujahidin* even after a UN agreement on the Soviet troop withdrawal. A month later every mainstream candidate in the US Presidential race was to give support to Reagan's unseemly attempt to force out of power the ruler of another American state, General Noriega of Panama, and in July, when over two hundred Iranian civilian passengers were killed in an attack by a US missile destroyer on an Iranair Airbus, few in the USA, apart from the ship's captain, saw fit to offer compensation, or compassion.

The greatest practical question hanging over the last two years of the Reagan Administration was whether there would be a direct attack on Nicaragua, an all-out invasion or a concerted air and sea attack in support of the *contras*. The possibility of this certainly existed, and there were those in the administration who favoured it: in the end, the Sandinistas remained in power albeit at the price of enormous economic and political concessions. Reagan failed to fulfil his promise *not* to leave the Central American crisis to his successor. In Afghanistan, a combination of US pressure and changing Soviet priorities led to the April 1988 agreement on a Soviet troop withdrawal. Elsewhere, there seemed less that the US could do to push its counter-revolutionary allies towards clinching victory, but a wide-ranging diplomatic process did begin. Of equal interest in assessing the Reagan Doctrine, however, was the evolution of

US policy in regard to threatened right-wing governments: the successes in 'finessing' revolutions seen by 1986 – in Sudan, El Salvador, Haiti, the Philippines and Korea – were not so easily repeated, as both the US administration and the oppositions in other countries discovered. Other, much tougher, allies faced problems comparable to the earlier five, but without an evidently available centrist alternative waiting in the wings: Chile, Paraguay, and, most important, Israel and South Africa.

The ruling groups in these right-wing dictatorships were less open to US pressure than elsewhere, and demonstrated just how limited and conditional was Reagan's support for democratic revolutions and national self-determination. In Pakistan, the challenge of the People's Party mounted when Benazir Bhutto returned in 1986 for a time was contained and the military régime of General Zia, sure of strategic support from the USA, remained in power until 1988. Only Zia's death in July 1988 allowed the opposition to win on terms acceptable to the armed forces, and to the US embassy. In Paraguay, as the long years of the Stroessner régime drew to a close, there was little sign of a major shift in régime policy: US military and economic aid to Paraguay was limited, and within the ruling *colorado* party the position of the traditionalist military leadership was now under pressure from a new-right faction of *militantes*. The pre-emptive coup of February 1989 was an attempt to preserve military rule. For Paraguay, the decisive external factor was the fate of democracy in neighbouring Argentina, more than pressure from a distant Washington. The régime of Pinochet in Chile remained equally intransigent, despite some resurgence of criticism from the USA and major economic problems at home: unfazed by his rejection in the referendum of September 1988, the dictator held on. In South Africa, the nationalist régime there had lost none of its resolve, despite the major uprisings of 1986 and 1987: if US policy now abandoned the policy of 'Constructive Engagement' pursued since the 1970s, it did little of substance to pressure the Botha régime. It confined itself to some symbolic economic gestures, and to seeking to manage the external dimensions of the South African crisis, by providing some aid to Mozambique, and to finding a diplomatic solution in Angola. For those in power in Seoul, Islamabad, Asunción, Santiago, Pretoria and Jerusalem, the 'Reagan Revolution' was less menacing than at first appeared. The recurrent popular mobilizations seen in four or five of these third world dictatorships (Paraguay being the exception) failed to reach the levels seen earlier in the Philippines and in Haiti. In Israel, the government remained secure in its strategic backing from the USA: despite the stamina of the Palestinian *intifadha* and Arab overtures, there was no slackening in the determination to prevent self-determination, and a Palestinian state.

If the historical verdict on the Reagan Doctrine has to be a mixed one, the analytic problems, the unravelling of why such a policy has been adopted and pursued in the first place, remain. One such analytic question has been alluded to already in respect of LIC: whether it should be seen as a *second-best*, a policy pursued because the most appropriate one, of direct attack, was not operable, or whether it was itself the *optimum* strategy for third world counter-revolution. An answer that would in part bridge these alternatives is that LIC, and the rhetoric surrounding it, was part of a policy of *erosion*, one designed to reduce domestic US resistance to third world intervention and so make the latter more acceptable. All three such explanations – the second-best, the optimal, and erosion – presuppose a degree of rationality and single-mindedness in the Administration with regard to foreign policy: yet here there is room for further debate about what the causes of the doctrine are. Given the permanently divided and competitive nature of the US foreign policy establishment, the doctrine could be seen not as a single rational strategy decided at the centre, so much as a piecemeal collection of initiatives produced by bureaucratic infighting and presidential whims. As the Iran-Contra affair showed, great divergences on foreign policy persisted within the Reagan Administration. In this sense, it was a simplification to talk of a 'Reagan Doctrine' at all, since there was no unifying coherence or even consistency in the various elements of the doctrine and no reason to believe that the doctrine as a whole was being implemented cogently in the final part of the Reagan Administration.

Beyond the bureaucratic conflicts of Washington, there lay the broader context of US public opinion, where the doctrine struck a chord and to which Reagan was always responsive and alert: the rhetoric about freedom, and the spectacular but militarily trivial attack on Libya in April 1986, had much to do with US domestic opinion, and less with implementing a coherent foreign policy. It is tempting, particularly for US writers critical of their country's foreign policy, to reduce foreign policy almost entirely to these domestic constraints and opportunities; and such a temptation is often misleading. But those searching for the coherence, and later fate, of the Reagan Doctrine may find it as much in these domestic factors as in any core strategy, enunciated or imputed, underlying Reagan's foreign policy.

These considerations apart, however, there lay one over-arching and inescapable context, one that prompted many of the Reagan initiatives as well as tempering their significance, and that was the Second Cold War as a whole, and the place of third world conflicts in it. LIC and the other strategies played a role in the confrontation with the USSR and in the US search for vulnerabilities on the other side. In the end it may well be here, in the east-west context as a whole rather than in US-third world relations, or the US domestic context, that the meaning and balance sheet of the Reagan Doctrine become clearest.

SOCIALISM ON THE DEFENSIVE: GORBACHEV'S RESPONSE

The evolution of US thinking on third world conflict during the 1980s coincided with a substantial change in Soviet thinking on this issue, and on its place in east-west relations as a whole. In the mid-1970s Soviet theory had stressed the positive and progressive character of third world revolution, and the Soviet role in promoting and defending it. But from the late 1970s onwards, a gradual process of rethinking became evident, through which Soviet writers and officials questioned the validity of third world revolution and qualified Soviet support. The first phase of this rethinking lasted from the later Brezhnev years, through the interregnum period up to 1985. The second was initiated by Gorbachev immediately upon taking office in February 1985, and was subsumed under the term 'new thinking'. In the second phase, new ideas about foreign affairs were proclaimed, without this explicitly contradicting the bases of earlier Soviet policy. It was only in the third phase of 'international *glasnost'*, which began in 1988, that foreign policy was subjected to the kind of criticism already being applied to domestic policy and that a wholesale rejection of the premises of Soviet conduct of external relations took place, including many of the assumptions upon which Soviet policy in the third world had been based. To set this third, disaffected and iconoclastic phase in perspective, it is necessary to go back to the apparent high point of Soviet policy in the third world, the end of the Brezhnev period.

Theories of Experience

In November 1982 Leonid Brezhnev was buried in Moscow, after an official farewell in Red Square. This occasion, the first state funeral of a Soviet leader since the death of Stalin in 1953, provided an opportunity to assess the state of the Soviet Union's alliances. Among the official mourners could be discerned four categories of leaders from socialist or radical states. First were representatives of ruling communist parties that formed part of the core Soviet bloc. Seven of these were from eastern Europe, but there were also representatives of six third world countries where power was held by pro-Soviet communists or by parties that in all but name were communist: Mongolia, Cuba, Vietnam, Laos, Cambodia and Afghanistan. Next came a category of countries which, while socialist, were not closely allied to the USSR: China and the DPRK (North Korea) fell into this grouping. Then there was a cluster of third world states which, while not communist, were considered to have a degree of commitment to the USSR: South Yemen, Ethiopia, Angola, Mozambique and Nicaragua. These were what Soviet theory termed 'states of socialist orientation', states which while not yet socialist were said to be preparing the ground for a transition to socialism. Finally, a wider grouping of third world states could be perceived, including over a dozen states that were regarded as filling the criteria of 'socialist orientation', but were not held in the same esteem as the leading five.[1]

The contrasts with Stalin's funeral nearly thirty years before were striking. On the one hand, the extent of Soviet influence and prestige in the world as a whole, and in the third world in particular, appeared to be greatly enhanced. In 1982 there were now eight ruling communist parties in the less developed world, as opposed to four in 1953 (Mongolia, China, Korea and Vietnam). Whereas Stalin had discounted the importance of third world nationalist and radical movements, and had scorned such nationalist leaders as Gandhi, Mosadeq and Nasser, the changes introduced after his death had allowed for the category of 'national-democratic', later 'socialist-oriented' states, and so expanded the potential number of Soviet allies to over twenty. The second (1958–1962) and third (1974–1980) waves of revolution, combined with changes in Soviet policy, had therefore shifted

Table Three

The Third World in Soviet Perspective 1982

1. *Core Communist Party Ruled States*
   Afghanistan
   Cambodia
   Cuba
   Laos
   Mongolia
   Vietnam

2. *Leading States of Socialist Orientation*
   Angola
   Ethiopia
   Mozambique
   Nicaragua
   South Yemen

3. *Independent Communist Party-Ruled States*
   China
   North Korea

4. *Less Advanced States of Socialist Orientation*
   Algeria
   Benin
   Burma
   Cape Verde
   Congo-Brazzaville
   Guinea
   Guinea Bissau
   Iraq
   Libya
   Madagascar
   Sao Tome
   Syria
   Tanzania
   Zimbabwe

5. *Marginal States of Socialist Orientation*
   Upper Volta (later Burkina Faso)
   Ghana
   Seychelles
   Surinam

the balance of forces in the third world to a significant degree in the direction of the USSR. In the decade up to 1982 the USSR had signed Treaties of Friendship and Co-operation with up to a dozen third world states.

Combined with this diplomatic and political extension, the overall strategic influence of the USSR had also greatly expanded: its naval forces were now present in the Indian Ocean, the Mediterranean and the Pacific, a far remove from the coastal defense force Stalin had maintained; its planes could provide emergency military aid to threatened allies in the third world, as far away as Vietnam, Ethiopia, Angola, and Cuba. In the latter half of the 1970s, the surge of international radical revolt had inflicted unprecedented damage on the USA's strategic system and shattered the illusion of *pax americana*, the idea that US hegemony could maintain a pro-western order throughout the third world in the aftermath of European colonial withdrawal.

It was hardly surprising, therefore, that one of the hallmarks of the late Brezhnev period was a certain pride and assertiveness about a new Soviet place in the third world. Just as Moscow had regarded the signing of the 1972 Strategic Arms Limitation Treaty with Washington as recognition of 'rough parity' in the field of nuclear weapon, so the enhanced Soviet position in the third world appeared to signal parity in Asia, Africa and Latin America. At the 1972 summit the Soviet side had secured US agreement for the signing of the Basic Principles, recognizing, in the Soviet interpretation, their respective roles in the third world, and on limiting the damage that third world crises could pose to east-west relations. Soviet strategy emphasized both components of this policy: on the one hand, as clearly stated in the new Soviet Constitution of 1977, the USSR was committed to aiding third world liberation movements; on the other hand, as Brezhnev argued at the Twenty-Fifth Congress of the CPSU in 1976 in the aftermath of Vietnam and Angola, support for revolution in the third world was not incompatible with detente.

The USSR now saw itself as a diplomatic actor in third world crises, pressing, in particular, its views on multilateral solutions to the problems of the Iran-Iraq war and the Arab-Israeli dispute. It was, at the same time, providing substantial military aid to third world allies, and its 'limited contingent' had entered Afghanistan in December 1979. Speaking at the Twenty-Sixth

Congress of the CPSU in February 1981 Brezhnev spoke of the favourable trend in world affairs: 'In economic and cultural development, and in improving social relations and socialist democracy – in literally all fields – world socialism is advancing steadily', he declared, going on to itemize Soviet assistance to 'newly-free countries', and in particular to the states of socialist orientation. He noted that the USSR had recently signed Treaties of Friendship and Co-operation with several of the socialist-oriented states: Angola, Ethiopia, Mozambique, Afghanistan, the PDRY, and Syria.[2] The revolution in Iran also received favourable mention, and he restated Soviet proposals for resolving the Gulf War and the Arab-Israeli dispute.

There was considerable validity in the claims Brezhnev made from the tribune of the Twenty Sixth CPSU Congress. In historical perspective, the international power of the Soviet Union, particularly with regard to the third world, had expanded more during his tenure than under any previous Soviet leader: in terms of the number of countries where he had assisted revolutionary forces sympathetic to the USSR to come to power, Brezhnev did more damage to the west than Khrushchev, Stalin or Lenin before him. But this apparently favourable trend had a negative side: the costs of these waves of third world revolution to the USSR were enormous, measured both by the negative impact they had on Soviet-US relations, and by the diversion of economic and military resources, which support of the infant socialist régimes entailed. These costs were already painful under Brezhnev, but concealed by the woolly rhetoric of his régime and the rush of successes in the late 1970s. They were to become much higher under his successors and to force, first under Andropov and then more clearly under Gorbachev, a substantial revision of Soviet strategies and thinking on the third world.

Despite the centralization of policy making in the CPSU, there has long been a wide range of thinking in Soviet writing on third world questions, and on the prospects for socialism in that domain.[3] In broad terms, however, Soviet official thinking on the third world had rested on two theoretical assumptions. The first was that world politics as a whole could be seen as a gradual transition from capitalism to socialism, that there was an underlying secular trend in favour of the USSR and its brand of socialism that would in the end prevail. Soviet thinking gave weight to a range of factors affecting relations between the two blocs – military, economic, political, ideological and cultural – and brought them together in the concept of the 'correlation of forces': in theory, the correlation was shifting gradually in the direction of the socialist camp, and advances in one component area, in, for example, nuclear capability or in economic performance, would enhance the overall adjustment of the 'correlation'.[4] From its beleagured position after the Bolshevik Revolution, when only the Mongolian People's Republic stood by it, the USSR had, after World War II, acquired eight new communist partners in eastern Europe and, over a longer period had seen its influence throughout the post-colonial world expand. Countries which had social revolutions were not all ripe for socialism, but after establishing the 'national democratic' foundations, they could in time begin the transition to socialism itself. Once they had gone a certain way along this path then such revolutions were at first assumed to be irreversible.

The second assumption, one rooted in Marx's own thinking, was that it was possible for less developed countries to begin a transition to socialism if they were assisted by more developed fraternal states. In Marx's own writings he had argued that a 'backward', still predominantly peasant Russia could attempt a socialist revolution if the proletariat in more developed countries, and in particular Germany, would take power and assist their Russian comrades. It was not necessary for states to go through all the phases of capitalist development, to pass through a period of resemblance to the UK or the USA, to begin the socialist transition. Transposed to Soviet thinking of the post-1953 period, this proposition entailed the view that, with the USSR's help, third world states that had not developed fully their capitalist potential could nonetheless begin the transition to socialism.

The conflict with the capitalist world was therefore a zero-sum game. Nuclear weapons prevented war between the two blocs from being inevitable, as earlier Leninist and Stalinist theory had suggested: but under the protective shroud of nuclear parity, the two blocs could and would compete in countries undergoing social and political upheaval. The task of the USSR was to do all it could to prevent a nuclear conflict with the USA, while at the same time providing assistance to these revolutionary movements so that they could take and hold power. This process would, in the long run, benefit the USSR and further weaken the west. To use Soviet terminology, the 'correlation of forces' was shifting inexorably in the direction of the Soviet bloc.

There were, however, major problems with the evaluation of Soviet third world relations propounded in the late Brezhnev era. In the first place, and despite the advances made in the number of states allied to the USSR, the Soviet Union remained much weaker in the third world than did the west. The votes in the UN on Afghanistan held every year after 1979 demonstrated that on this, the most sensitive of all great power issues in the 1980's, the USSR could count on the support of at most fourteen third world states, as compared to over one hundred voting with the USA and many others abstaining.[5] In the military sphere, the USSR had certainly expanded its capabilities, but from a very low base: its overall strength in the third world was far less than that of the USA. It had no aircraft carriers capable of launching combat aircraft: it could not even have matched the UK, which in 1982 fought a carrier-based campaign 8,000 miles from its own frontiers against Argentina. It had a presence in the Pacific and Indian Oceans, but this was a far less commanding naval force than the combined Western fleet. The number of its military bases outside the Warsaw Pact area was a fraction of the USA's and its allies'. The development of more rapid and mobile strike-formations by the USA in the 1980s lengthened this lead. In economic terms, the situation was even less favourable. The USSR was providing economic aid to third world allies, and to many countries, such as Pakistan, Morocco and Turkey, that were hostile to it. But in comparative terms, and in terms of quality, Soviet aid was greatly inferior to what the west could offer. When the third world countries in the Group of 77 or the Non-Aligned Movement called for reform of the international economic system, they turned to the USA, other large OECD countries, and the international economic institutions they dominated – not to the USSR. If there had, in official Soviet terms, been a change in the correlation of forces, the overall balance was still indisputably in favour of the west.

This unfavourable reckoning was matched by precariousness and unreliable balance within the bloc of pro-Soviet states themselves. Indeed, if the 1953–1982 period had seen a net increase in the number of states allied to the USSR, it had provided more than enough evidence of the reversibility of such states' alignments. It could not be taken for granted that once states had acquired communist régimes or had begun the phase of socialist orientation, all would be well thereafter. In the first place, communist parties themselves had proven to be less than reliable allies of the USSR. In eastern Europe, Yugoslavia had shown the way, by successfully defying Stalin in 1948. Under Khrushchev, the Soviet bloc sustained its greatest loss when China broke away in 1963, subtracting from the Soviet alliance system a quarter of the world's population: after a decade of defiance of the USSR and the USA from a left-radical position, China proceeded to form a loose alliance with Washington. Chinese influence on the international communist movement as a whole was limited; but in the Far East the rivalry with China had profound effects on Soviet relations with other states, including communist ones. The conflicts in Korea and in Indo-China, hitherto straight east-west contests, now acquired an even more agonized, triangular character. In the early 1970s, the DPRK moved to an uneasy middle position between Moscow and Peking. In late 1978, less than four years after it had defeated the Saigon government, Vietnam cascaded into war with Cambodia.

Moscow's situation in the states of socialist orientation was in many ways equally precarious. Here there emerged not only the prospect of a break with the USSR, but something worse – a return to capitalism: the transition to socialism in the third world was not, therefore, irreversible. If China was the outstanding disappointment amongst the third world communist countries, it was almost matched by a parallel setback involving the most important national-democratic or socialist-oriented state, namely Egypt. Under Khrushchev, Egypt had been held up as the model national democratic state, an anti-imperialist régime based on state reforms and popular mobilization, that would, in time, begin a transition to socialism. Nasserite Egypt represented for Khrushchev's third world policy in the 1950s and early 1960s what Kuomintang China had represented for the USSR in the middle 1920s, a 'progressive' military-nationalist régime within which a communist movement could play an independent, and

increasingly powerful role. Through Soviet military and economic aid, Egypt had been the outstanding example of Soviet
support for nationalist régimes in the third world. The USSR
along with Egypt claimed credit for forcing Britain, France and
Israel to withdraw their forces after they had invaded Egypt
in 1956. But the relationship with Egypt had always involved
tensions: Nasser had ruled through a military apparatus and
had kept the Egyptian communist movement in subservience,
imprisoning and at times killing its members. Nasser had always
distinguished his 'Arab socialism' from the 'scientific socialism'
of the USSR, arguing that in two key respects his programme
was not comparable: Arab socialism was of religious, in this case
Islamic inspiration, whereas scientific socialism was materialist;
Arab socialism did not believe in primitive socialist accumulation, in forcing austerity on the masses in one generation in order
to accelerate economic development. On the strategic front, the
USSR had always made a much more cautious estimate of
Egyptian military capabilities than had Nasser himself. In 1967,
miscalculating his own abilities, Nasser gave Israel the opening
to launch a devastating war. The Egyptian state survived, after
international pressure brought Israel to a halt: but the myth of
Egyptian might was shattered, and with Nasser's death in 1970
the experiment of 'Arab socialism' was brought to an end. After
using Soviet military aid to fight a comparatively successful war
in October 1973, Nasser's successor Sadat opened the country
to private capital, reoriented its foreign policy to the west, and
broke the alliance with the USSR.

The lessons of Egypt were of much wider relevance to Soviet
thinking on the third world. In the first place, they showed that
national democratic régimes would not necessarily proceed in
stages to socialism. Some were precarious military or populist
régimes which by failing to consolidate their hold on the state
apparatus and to meet popular demands would themselves be
overthrown by right-wing forces. This occurred in Indonesia
(1965), Mali (1965), Ghana (1966) and Chile (1973). Others
were régimes that saw the 'socialist' or state-dominated period
not as a transition to a more complete socialism but as an
interim before a fuller restoration of market economics and
political pluralism. In the words of one Soviet critic of socialist
oriented states:

In a number of young states the public sector is poorly managed, with incompetent, corrupt technocrats in charge, and has little in common with social (that is people's) property. Many of the enterprises in this sector have been placed in the service of private business (which means, in effect, stimulating the growth of the domestic bourgeoisie at society's expense); they provide technocrats and bureaucrats with cushy jobs and are hatcheries of a bureaucratic bourgeoisie, models of mismanagements and objects of plunder.[6]

This had occurred long before in Turkey, which was in all but name a socialist-oriented state of the interwar years: the period of Kemalist *étatisme* initiated in the 1920s, based on state control of the economy, a one party system, and a neutral position vis-a-vis the USSR gave way, once the régime had consolidated itself, to the opening of the 1950s, and the emergence of a multiparty system, however unstable, a more unregulated capitalist economy and Turkish entry into NATO. In Egypt too, the Nasserite period had created a new ruling class that took the country back to capitalism in a fuller sense. The rightward slippage without major political upheaval of several other such states –Sudan after 1971, Somalia after 1976, Iraq after 1978, Guinea after the death of Sekou Touré in 1984 – indicated that a capitalist re-orientation could happen just as easily through this gradual and continuous process as it could through a violent break, with a military coup.

This inherent danger of defection within communist and socialist-oriented states in the third world was not the only difficulty that the bloc's expansion presented. Often of equal concern to the USSR was a contagion within the most apparently loyal of states, the tendency to excess of zeal and 'adventurism'. The break between China and the USSR in 1963 grew out of a long history of disputes on revolutionary strategy covering the period from the mid-1920s to the Chinese communist assumption of power in 1949, as well as domestic policy in the 1950s. While third world revolutionary movements have looked to the USSR for support and models, and have to a considerable extent proclaimed loyalty to the USSR, this appearance of subordination has in many instances been misleading. Indigenous radical traditions, nationalist sentiments and local calculations have all tempted Soviet allies to pursue policies seen by the USSR as 'left deviations', as too radical or precipitate. Some of these were internal programmes , and in particular radical measures imposed from above that alienated the population. Soviet criticism of the Chinese Great Leap Forward was a striking instance of this, as was official scepticism about the Guevarist economic policies pursued by Cuba in the 1960s. The imposition of social reforms by the PDPA in Afghanistan after 1978 was another dramatic case, not least because it led to the critical situation in which Soviet forces had to intervene to try and stabilize the situation. In other countries too – in Ethiopia and South Yemen, for example – Soviet advice was directed as much against premature reforms as in favour of specific transformative measures.

If Soviet and third world allies disagreed on the correct pace of internal reform, they also clashed on international policy. While the USSR was always concerned at the extent to which such states might soften opposition to the west, and even, in the Egyptian way, slip towards new allegiances and hostility towards the Soviet Union, it was also alive to the opposite danger, of adventurist international policies. Both Soviet and western writers have sustained the illusion that third world revolutionaries, and particularly third world communist parties, have acted at the behest of Moscow in all major foreign policy initiatives. The reality has been rather different. The catalogue of these conflicts is also the actual record of much of the Soviets' relations with the third world: the Korean communists, led by Kim Il Sung, launched their invasion of the south in June 1950, in the hope of capturing and reuniting the whole country before the USA could respond.[7] Instead, the USA organized an international intervention force that drove the Korean communists back and provoked the most sanguinary conflict of the first Cold War. The Chinese communists escalated the conflict with Taiwan in 1958–9 at the moment when Khrushchev was trying to improve relations with the USA, and then broke with Moscow over the question of nuclear war. The Cubans during the 1962 missile crisis opposed Moscow's compromise with Washington, and refused to allow international inspection of sites on the island. Once he had obtained an informal undertaking from the USA that it would not invade the island, Castro was able to encourage guerrilla movements in Latin America, thereby defying not only the USA but also the USSR, whose own allies in the region, in shape of the official communist parties, opposed Cuban revolutionary strategy: the divergences that were to emerge between Havana and Moscow after 1985 were to echo some of these earlier disagreements. The Vietnamese, despairing of a political resolution of the division of their country, decided in 1960 to relaunch guerrilla warfare in the south: this decision was taken against Soviet advice, but after the break with China in 1963 and the introduction of US combat forces in 1965 the USSR was compelled to alter its stance and make a firm commitment to the Vietnamese NLF.

This autonomy in foreign policy was also evident in the conduct of some of the states of socialist orientation. Nasser's blunder in 1967, which led to the Israeli victory, was one classic example, involving as it did an underestimation of the enemy and overvaluation of his own forces. Kadhafi's foreign policy, including support for terrorist groups, intervention in neighbouring Chad, reckless demagogy towards other Arab régimes and unsustainable maritime claims, was another case of reckless behaviour from a weak position. An equally truculent ally in the 1970s was the régime in Aden, that of the People's Democratic Republic of Yemen: while Moscow provided substantial wherewithal for the PDRY to defend itself against attack, Aden was also urged to 'normalize' relations with the three neighbours, Saudi Arabia, Oman and the Yemen Arab Republic with which it was chronically in dispute. The PDRY adopted this course only in 1982 when the opposition movements it had supported in Oman and the YAR were defeated and it faced mounting socio-economic problems at home.[7] Underlying much Soviet assessment of Arab states' foreign policies generally has been the belief that their declarations, particularly vis-a-vis Israel, have lacked realism or the ability to transform words into action.

For the USSR such initiatives by third world states, at home and abroad, have carried two great risks. The first is that by overreaching themselves and by provoking resistance these states will endanger their own survival: the diverse adventurisms of Nasserite Egypt and PDPA Afghanistan were clear enough examples of this. In 1983 of course, one Soviet ally – the socialist-oriented state of Grenada – was to show how, as a result of an outbreak of factionalism within the ruling party, and consequent brutality against the population, the door was opened to a US intervention that was welcomed by the majority of the islanders. The second risk was that by provoking international crises, these states would draw in the USSR and increase the risk of nuclear war. The Soviet view, often repeated, was that these third world states underestimated the dangers of nuclear war and pursued foreign policies that placed not only their own régimes but also those of allied states in jeopardy. From the disputes with Peking and Havana over nuclear weapons in the early 1960s onwards, this remained a permanent source of Soviet anxiety about third world allies.

In addition to their continued relative weakness in the third world, and the unreliability of third world allies, two other issues underlined the costs to the USSR of its new role. Nuclear war was avoided, but it is a matter of record that, crises over Berlin apart, most of the nuclear confrontations in the postwar period occurred in the third world: Korea, Cuba, Vietnam and the Arab-Israeli dispute. In addition, these disputes came, from the middle of the 1970s onwards, to play a more prominent role in Soviet-US relations and were increasingly seen as a source of continued tension between them. Whatever Soviet officials believed about the legitimacy of the movements involved, and of Soviet aid to them, the fact was that the price of such support in east-west terms rose considerably. After many other disputes, détente came to an end in 1979, amidst the turmoil of Afghanistan, and from the early 1980s onwards US support for opposition forces within Soviet third world allies began to take its toll. The Afghan intervention was the most obviously costly and, within the USSR, controversial of these commitments: but the overall policy, dating back to Khrushchev's period, of backing third world revolutions and nationalist movements as part of a global rivalry with the USA appeared to be increasingly difficult.

The difficulties lay not only in the US response, but in the growing conflict between the commitment to the third world and the needs of the USSR itself. In the 1960s and 1970s there was considerable, unofficial, criticism of Soviet third world policy within the USSR because this was associated with consumer goods and food shortages at home. The USSR was believed to be sending goods and money to third world states at the expense of domestic consumers, and popular resentment, of an often racist hue, grew accordingly. With the deterioration in Soviet-US relations in the late 1970s, and the return of the Cold War proper, these third world states were blamed ever more directly for the difficulties facing the USSR: the policies of Vietnamese, Cubans, Afghans, Arabs and the like were charged by Soviet public opinion with the worsening of the country's relations with the USA. The official response to this problem was more muted, but Soviet economic aid was an eloquent indication of Soviet priorities. According to western estimates, over 80% of Soviet economic aid to the third world went to the core communist allies. The advice to states of socialist orientation was that, while the USSR could supply some economic aid, they had to seek the majority of their economic support elsewhere. If the constraints of Soviet domestic economy were evident in the Brezhnev period itself, and in the Soviet inability to meet the economic needs of socialist-oriented allies, this conflict was to become even starker in subsequent years, with the advent of Gorbachev to power. One of the main consequences of *perestroika* was to strain even more the relation between the consolidation of socialism in the USSR and its extension abroad. Now even the political and strategic interests of the USSR

Table 4

Soviet economic aid to third world
(in US $m)

	1983	% 1983
Cuba	500	17.1
Vietnam	1025	35.1
Afghanistan	312	10.7
Cambodia	110	3.8
Laos	38	1.3
Mongolia	620	21.3
Total States ruled by communist parties	2605	89.3
Others	312	10.7
TOTAL	2917	100

Source: OECD

were understood to be at odds with the hitherto prevailing norms of internationalist commitment. The consolidation of socialism involved not so much a progressive realignment of the global correlation of forces, as an intensive reorganization of the USSR itself.

The process of Soviet rethinking on the third world, reflected both in theoretical writing and in policy, had begun well before Gorbachev himself came to power.[8] As early as the mid-1970s doubts began to be expressed by Soviet writers about the general lines of the Khrushchev strategy, and greater care was taken to specify the political mechanisms by which regressions of the Egyptian kind could be avoided. In the later Brezhnev years, Soviet diplomacy paid particular attention to attempts to negotiate on third world crises with the USA: some, such as unpublicized understandings on the Horn of Africa in 1978, worked reasonably well, but there was no US willingness to accept formal bilateral or multilateral negotiation on major third world questions. Brezhnev's speech at the 1981 CPSU Congress, although generally upbeat, was in some respects more reserved than in 1976, and, he did not repeat the by then rather unrealistic view that internationalist activity by the USSR in the third world *would not* weaken détente. Under Andropov, the limits on Soviet aid to socialist-oriented states were clearly spelt out. In a major speech in June 1983, Andropov emphasized that the states of socialist orientation would have to rely mainly on their own resources. Proclaiming socialism was one thing, he said, actually building and achieving it was something else. Andropov did not, like Brezhnev, exalt the national liberation movements, and he stressed the need for economic rather than military competition between the two camps. Many of the ideas that were to shape Gorbachev's approach to the third world were already, therefore, rooted in Soviet policy.

While this rethinking was taking place in Moscow itself, revision of entrenched ideas was also under way in many of the allied states, especially of economic strategy. In these countries, there were substantial shifts away from more centralized models well before the USSR itself began, from 1985 onwards, to liberalize its own economy. Thus in the PDRY a greater measure of freedom for the private sector and greater tolerance of emigration was initiated in 1980. In Cuba an experiment with the free market for some agricultural produce began in 1981. In Mozambique there was a marked shift in policy after the Fourth Congress of FRELIMO in 1983. In the Mongolian Peoples' Republic the new Secretary-General Batmunkh began to liberalize in 1984. In Vietnam some encouragement of private farming and the service sector was evident from 1979 onwards.

These changes in the policy of the socialist camp represented a significant departure from the more optimistic and mechanistic approaches of the earlier Brezhnev period. Indeed, third world policy was one of the first areas of official Soviet theory to feel the cutting edge of new thinking. In this regard, the analogy with China is striking. Whilst Chinese domestic policy continued very much along orthodox lines during the 1970s and had to await the death of Mao in 1976 for substantial revision, the big change in foreign policy had come in 1971–1972, with the opening to the USA, and the shift in third world policy away from support for third world revolution and towards a united 'anti-hegemonist' front of states. The shift in Soviet policy was not so dramatic: but it is striking how, in both cases, a new foreign orientation had its roots under an earlier régime and how, in its later development, it was so interlocked with a process of domestic revitalization.

'New Thinking' and Regional Crises

The interim between the death of Brezhnev in November 1982 and the election of Gorbachev in February 1985 marked a period of transition in Soviet policy as a whole, domestic as well as international. Andropov's brief tenure had given indications of a desire to break with old policies, notably on the third world. With Gorbachev installed there appeared to be a rapid transformation of Soviet policy, as revealed in official statements and expositions of Soviet views. From the April 1985 Plenum of the Central Committee of the CPSU, the first occasion for an official statement of policy, Gorbachev himself became a tireless expositor of what he termed 'new thinking' in the international sphere, and used the Twenty Seventh Congress of the CPSU in March 1986 to introduce a new Programme of the Party, the first since Khrushchev's of 1961. Whereas between 1980 and 1984 there had been no summit meetings of US and Soviet leaders, there were four such encounters in the period from November 1985 (Geneva) to May 1988 (Moscow), and a fifth, brief, meeting in December 1988 (New York). In addition to progress on nuclear weapons, epitomized in the INF agreement of May 1988, there was also active discussion of third world issues, or what were now termed 'regional questions', at the summits and in other meetings of officials. A new era of Soviet-US relations with the third world seemed to have dawned.

The rethinking of Soviet policy on the third world drew, as we have seen, on the changes already maturing under Brezhnev and his immediate successors, but were also a product of the broader 'new thinking' on the international arena. The first such innovation was Gorbachev's statement, contrasting with the hitherto prevailing primacy of class struggle, that the common interests of mankind should prevail over differences between social and political systems. In the 1950s Khrushchev had initiated a process of rethinking on this, by arguing for a degree of peaceful coexistence and the avoidance of nuclear war, but he had continued to insist on the importance of a combative competition between the socialist and capitalist camps. The 1961 CPSU Programme projected a vision of long-run economic and political contest with the west. While not denying that elements of conflict persisted, Gorbachev laid much greater stress on the universal interests of humanity, and on the shared dangers they faced, from nuclear war to ecological decay. Gorbachev recognized that class conflict had always been the basis of the Marxist view of politics, but that the advent of nuclear weapons had altered this: 'Now, with the emergence of weapons of mass, that is, universal destruction, there appeared an objective limit for class confrontation in the international arena: the threat of universal destruction. For the first time ever there emerged a real, not speculative and remote, common human interest – to save humanity from disaster.' This led Gorbachev 'to a new philosophy of peace and to the comprehension of new dialectics of the common human and class interest and principles in our modern epoch'.[9] In arguing for this, Gorbachev adopted the term current in much western liberal thinking of the 1970s, 'interdependence'. Whereas Khrushchev had seen the conflict of capitalism and socialism as the central question in world affairs, Gorbachev had a distinctly different view:

> We have seen the main issue – the growing tendency towards interdependence of the states of the world community. Such are the dialectics of present-day development. The world – contradictory, socially and politically diverse, but nonetheless interconnected and largely integral – is forming with great difficulties, as if it is feeling its way through a conflict of opposites . . . Here we see our interdependence, the integrity of the world, the imperative need for pooling the efforts of humanity for the sake of its self-preservation, for its benefit today, tomorrow and for all time.[10]

This theoretical revision of the basis of international conflict went together with a new stress on the resolution of international issues through negotiation and compromise. This applied in the nuclear field, where the USSR from 1985 onwards made unprecedented concessions in the areas of weapons destruction and verification, abandoning negotiating positions it had sustained for much of the 1970s and early 1980s. The new Soviet policy also accorded much greater importance to international institutions such as the UN, seen as the forum for implementing policies of benefit to all mankind. Thus Gorbachev not only paid the USSR's financial contribution to the UN, but also proposed a return to activities envisaged in the original charter of 1945 that had long been buried by the conflicts of the Cold War: first amongst these being the Military Committee envisaged in Chapter VII. At the same time, the new Soviet foreign policy sought to break down barriers to negotiation with other states that had existed for years or even decades. While pursuing an active dialogue with the USA, the Soviet Union sought to improve relations 'with all countries, large and small'. A new attempt was made to have a separate dialogue with Europe, around the slogan of 'a common European home', and to open discussion with a range of third world countries with which the USSR had always had hostile relations, or indeed none at all: South Korea, Indonesia, Saudi Arabia, Israel, even, at an unofficial level, with South Africa. Most important of all, Moscow sought to improve relations with China, the country that was most central to its foreign policy after the USA. In

December 1988 the Chinese Foreign Minister visited Moscow for the first such high-ranking meeting in nearly thirty years, and as each of the two major socialist states encountered difficulties with its economic and political system, they increasingly came to appreciate the common character of the problems each of them faced.

These general alterations in international outlook went together with a rethinking of Soviet policy towards the states of the socialist camp. Here there was an uneasy combination of two themes in Soviet policy. On the one hand, the USSR under Gorbachev now abandoned the position espoused by Brezhnev: this involved ditching not only the 'Brezhnev Doctrine' in the strict sense, which gave the USSR the right to intervene militarily in socialist states if the system was supposedly under threat, but also the broader inter-communist policy of encouraging socialist countries to imitate the USSR in their internal political and social orders. Gorbachev espoused diversity within the communist movement, and even upbraided fraternal parties and governments for adopting a too sycophantic, or as he put it 'sugar-coated' attitude to the USSR. At the same time, however, Gorbachev sought to introduce into relations between communist parties and states the same note of businesslike directness and *perestroika* that he was advocating in the USSR. This involved not only inter-state and inter-party relations as such, but also the internal workings of these countries. Now that the Soviet Union itself was facing up to many of its internal failings and to the gap between rhetoric and reality, and was acknowledging how difficult socialist transformation really was, the socialist-oriented states were not to be allowed to remain immune from such reassessment.

The contradictory result of 'new thinking' was that just as the USSR was urging its allies to pursue more independent paths, it was also stimulating in them a response to developments in the USSR itself. In November 1987, for example, the Soviet leadership held a two-day seminar in Moscow for the delegations of communist and socialist parties attending the seventieth anniversary of the Bolshevik revolution. Great prominence was given to representatives of socialist parties who were encouraged to join with the USSR in the new foreign policy initiatives, and to overcome the division between socialist and communist parties that had begun in 1914, and which communists, following Lenin's injunctions, had done as much as anyone to sustain. This was a theme repeated in a speech on 12 April 1988 by Anatoli Dobrynin, now head of the international department of the CPSU secretariat, at a meeting of over Ninety pro-Soviet communist parties held in Prague, the first such gathering since 1969. It amounted to a major shift in the international orientation of the CPSU. For the communist and socialist-oriented parties in power, however, there were other equally important messages: since they had imitated the Soviet model of the Brezhnevite period, and suffered from many shortcomings, which the USSR had often to help in solving, they too should learn from *perestroika* and introduce reforms in their economies, political systems and foreign policies. Lest these ruling parties should not have heard the message clearly enough, Soviet envoys to third world socialist states began, for the first time ever, to make critical observations in public about the economic and social performance of their allies: in Afghanistan, Cuba, Nicaragua and the PDRY, such criticism came as an unwelcome surprise to local officials, as must have the abrasive discussion of socialist-oriented and other third world states in the Soviet press itself.[11]

One other message came across loud and clear from the November 1987 seminar, and from other Soviet declarations: for the USSR the overriding concern in the forthcoming period was internal reform. Third world and eastern European allies were reminded that the USSR was concentrating its economic resources on domestic change, and that Moscow needed more normal and harmonious relations with the west in order to pursue its restructuring. The USSR could not bear the financial or strategic costs which it had sustained for much of the post-war period, and the allies of the USSR should support it in this by better use of their own resources, by political transformation, and by conducting more active and flexible foreign policies themselves. The Soviet message was, therefore, doubly disconcerting; it both announced that these countries were responsible for themselves and called on them to follow the Soviet lead.

This policy of projecting 'the international significance of *perestroika*' reflected the degree to which 'new thinking' on foreign policy was a reflection of internal Soviet concerns. Above all, perhaps, Gorbachev challenged the view, long assumed in

Soviet statements, of the irreversibility of socialist revolutions: in his speech at the end of the Twenty Seventh CPSU Congress he had warned of the dangers of revolutions failing, and, if this applied to the USSR itself, it was even more germane to Moscow's third world allies. Not only the direction but the very content and style of the new foreign policy reflected changes within the USSR. The model of a socialist polity being projected to other communist and socialist-oriented states differed markedly from that of the Brezhnev period. there were to be fewer bombastic claims, presentations of medals and assertions of socialist advance, and more recognition of failings and of the diversity of views within party and régime. Even more significantly, in 1988 the critique of Brezhnev's years of 'stagnation' was extended to foreign policy. Under what was termed 'international *glasnost*', it became possible to argue that some of the international, including third world, initiatives of the Brezhnev period had been mistaken. There had, it was claimed, been too great a stress on military at the expense of political factors, and opportunities for compromise and negotiation had been missed. Thus the tenth thesis contained in the motions presented to the CPSU Conference in June 1988 cast doubt on the achievements of earlier leaders:

A critical analysis of the past has been made to show that our foreign policy, too, has not escaped dogmatic and subjective attitudes. It trailed behind the fundamental changes occurring in the world and missed new opportunities to reduce tensions and enhance understanding among nations. In our bid for military-strategic parity, we sometimes failed to use the opportunities available to attain security for our nation by political means, and as a result, allowed ourselves to be lured into an arms race, which could not but affect our country's social and economic progress and its position on the international scene'.[12]

Other Soviet writers spoke of the damage done by third world policy to the USSR and to relations with the west. No examples were given, but Afghanistan was certainly a prime candidate for this list, and in other contexts Soviet officials were now able to state that they had opposed the decision to send troops to Afghanistan in 1979.

Specific examples aside, this trend of foreign-policy revision made a generic claim that third world commitments had cost the USSR too dearly and conflicted with long-run Soviet interests. Indeed, such was the spirit of retrospective criticism that it seemed as if all responsibility for the difficulties of the late 1970s and early 1980s rested on Soviet shoulders alone. There seemed to be a strange unwillingness on the part of Soviet officials to see how far the USA and its allies had made their own contribution to the Second Cold War. At the same time, such was the lassitude about international issues that the long-established Soviet commitment to promoting the cause of socialism on a world scale seemed to have been eroded. In a poll of senior Soviet diplomats and international affairs specialists published in August 1988, no less than 77% of those asked responded that the idea of spreading socialism was out of date as a policy aim.[3] The implications for the third world were far-reaching and, for Soviet allies, potentially unsettling. Third world states did not fear the economic reforms being introduced in the USSR, except insofar as they were accompanied by tighter accounting and a reduced outflow of Soviet development funds. But the political changes that went with them, and the overriding stress on accommodation with the USA, meant that many in the third world felt themselves to be endangered.

Gorbachev and the Third World: Four Policies

The implications of 'new thinking' for the third world were many-sided, as we have already suggested, but after the first four years of Gorbachev's rule it was possible to pick out some policies that were of particular relevance for Soviet attitudes to third world conflict, and for the ways in which the USSR might attempt some resolution of them. If these were stated in a cautious form during the initial 1985–1988 phase of 'new thinking', they were more explicitly presented with the advent of 'international *glasnost*' in 1988. Distinctive and innovative as these policies were, however, they did not simply represent an alternative and fully-formed set of ideas which the new Soviet leader brought into office with him in February 1985. On the one hand, as already noted, many of the trends and elements present in 'new thinking' had been maturing in Soviet writing and even in official Soviet policy over the previous few years. On the other hand, what was obvious in domestic policy was also evident in foreign policy, namely that Gorbachev's ideas went on changing after he came to power: ideas about new Soviet democracy and of *perestroika* being a 'second revolution' only emerged in 1987 and 1988, as did proposals for the restoration of individual rights and the separation of state and party; similarly, in international affairs, it took time for 'new thinking' to evolve, as evidenced by the fact that only in 1988 did it become possible openly to debate and criticize Soviet foreign policy.

When Gorbachev came to office the immediate problem he faced was that the USSR was involved in several third world military conflicts and that these commitments were impeding an improvement of Soviet-US relations. Within a short period, he launched a series of initiatives on the third world in the hope of reducing, if not ending, these conflicts. Thus by April 1988 he had signed an agreement under UN auspices to withdraw Soviet forces from Afghanistan, and had already, in July 1987, through Security Council Resolution 598, joined with the other four permanent members of the UN Security Council to urge a compromise peace on Iran and Iraq. Soviet diplomats were busy seeking ways of improving relations with China and were discussing with them and the other interested parties not only a resolution of the Cambodian question but also that of Korea. In a major speech in Vladivostok in July 1986 Gorbachev proposed a new diplomatic settlement for the Pacific region, comparable to the Helsinki process in Europe: for Gorbachev the Asia-Pacific region within which he included the USA was the hub of the contemporary world, and, in part, explained the Soviet decision to establish contact with the ROK (South Korea) and participate in the 1988 Seoul Olympics, despite DPRK appeals for a boycott. The USSR was also active in trying to convene an international conference on the Arab-Israeli question and was encouraging a compromise settlement over Angola and Namibia. These specific initiatives reflected some underlying developments in Soviet thinking as a whole.

(i) *Demilitarization*

The first of these conciliatory policies, demilitarization, involved a reduced emphasis on the role of force in international relations, and in particular in the third world. Parallel to Soviet moves in arms talks with the USA and western Europe, where it made substantial, indeed disproportionate concessions to attain agreement, the USSR advocated a demilitarization of the third world. The USA and the USSR should withdraw forces stationed there, and should cease using inter-state conflicts in the third world as the occasion for increasing their military forces there. In the words of one senior Soviet foreign policy expert, Yevgeni Primakov:

> As for the external factors of regional conflicts, their impact could be drastically weakened or even eliminated altogether by introducing certain 'rules of conduct' into the practice of the great powers. First of all, they should stop using such conflicts as a reason and sometimes as a pretext for increasing their military presence in a particular region. Incidentally, that is precisely why regional conflict situations tend to become part of the confrontation on a global level.
>
> The Soviet Union has taken the firm decision to scale down its military presence abroad. It expresses the readiness to give up the stationing of Soviet armed forces on foreign territory provided that the USA displays a similar readiness.[14]

Nor was this reassessment of military policies confined to cases where Soviet arms had arguably exacerbated conflicts. By late 1988 Soviet writers and officials could be heard arguing that no third world conflict had ever been resolved by force, a thesis rather different from saying that force alone had not resolved them. This assertion must have come as a surprise to many state leaders in the third world, not least in Vietnam, Algeria, Angola and Nicaragua.

(ii) *National Reconciliation*

This first component of the revised Soviet approach was of special relevance to conflicts between states – India and Pakistan, Iran and Iraq, Israel and the Arabs. But it also applied to the second component, the stress on 'national reconciliation', that is on compromises between the parties involved in civil wars *within* third world countries. The idea of 'national reconciliation' marked a significant break from previous Soviet orthodoxy, which had cast most if not all third world civil wars as conflicts between progressive and counter-revolutionary forces, with the implication being that the latter had, in one way or another, to be defeated. Despite occasional references to the need to find 'political' solutions to such conflicts, the overwhelming weight of Soviet policy, both declarative and practical, had been on military solutions. In the new mood of 'national reconciliation' established Soviet-supported régimes were urged to open negotiations with opposition forces, and to seek to form coalitions with them. In 1986 the USSR encouraged and probably engineered a change in the leadership at the Nineteenth Plenum of the Central Committee of the PDPA in Kabul, after which the new secretary-general Najibullah proclaimed a policy of 'national reconciliation', offering a ceasefire and talks with the Afghan rebels. In Cambodia, the Phnom Penh government began in 1987 to hold direct talks with Prince Sihanouk, leader of the three-party opposition alliance. In the same year the Nicaraguan government opened negotiations with the contras. In the Arab-Israeli context, Soviet diplomacy worked for dialogue between Palestinians and Israelis, while, at the same, assiduously trying to promote greater unity amongst the factionalized Palestinian groups themselves. This policy reflected the belief that after a decade or so of fighting these régimes could not prevail over their opponents by military means, but also that by opening such talks and declaring their willingness to compromise the embattled allies could reduce external involvement in their countries' internal conflicts.

(iii) *Multilateral Reopenings*

If the first component of 'new thinking' in the third world was addressed to the USA, and the second to Soviet allies, the third was addressed to other states who could play a significant role in regional issues – including states that had, in an earlier period, been seen as hostile. Active relations with non-socialist and even right-wing governments in the third world were certainly not a new element in Soviet foreign policy. Under Brezhnev, the USSR had enjoyed good relations with such conservative leaders as the King of Morocco and the military junta of Argentina, not to mention Idi Amin of Uganda. In more than one case, Moscow had found itself pursuing 'correct' and even warm relations with régimes that were about to be overthrown by their own enraged subjects: thus it had welcomed Haile Selassie to Moscow in 1973, less than a year before the commencement of the Ethiopian revolution; it had recognized and maintained relations with the Lon Nol régime in Cambodia, up to its overthrow in May 1975; a matter of weeks before the successful popular uprising in the Philippines in February 1976, it was welcoming Imelda Marcos in Moscow. A similar perversity could be detected in the European arena where, following the revelation that Austrian president and former UN Secretary-General Kurt Waldheim had been associated with Nazi atrocities in the Balkans, Moscow rushed in to assure him of Soviet support and to congratulate him on fighting off a 'Zionist' conspiracy. Such policies were, in the main, as much a product of diplomatic inertia and strategy opportunism as of a longer-run policy but under 'new thinking' a more coherent and consistent policy of initiatives was introduced. Thus improved relations with Israel and China, in particular, represented an innovative and systematic approach absent from the pre-1985 period, an approach that was also evident in Gorbachev's intention to visit Latin America in 1989 or 1990 and in warmer relations with Saudi Arabia and the ASEAN states.

These diplomatic offensives towards capitalist states in the less developed world rested upon at least two other significant considerations. One was diplomatic experience: the USSR had found that in many cases third world capitalist states, not committed to reproducing the socialist transition and its associated rhetorical excesses, or to 'sugar-coated' exchanges of greetings with the CPSU leadership, had been more reliable and less dangerous allies than their more wordy revolutionary counterparts.

Prominent amongst such countries was India, a country which, under the Congress Party of Nehru, had occasionally been classified as 'socialist', but which was in reality a major, and in some respects flourishing capitalist state. The Soviet alliance with India, which had substantial economic and cultural dimensions as well as a military component, was a model of stability in Soviet-third world relations, compared to Moscow's dealings with China, Egypt or Cuba. In the Middle East too, the USSR had over a considerable period of time developed relations with Arab monarchies that were, while never 'fraternal', steadier and more beneficial than relations with Iraq or Libya: thus with Jordan and Kuwait the USSR had been able to maintain good relations, including the supply of arms, despite their ties to the USA and their rather blatantly non-socialist forms of government.

It was, in retrospect, one of the ironies of Soviet foreign policy in the 1960s and early 1970s that Moscow had benefitted greatly from consolidating relations with two other, non-Arab, monarchies on the sensitive southern frontier, only to find these accommodating rulers swept away: the consequences of the fall of these two neighbours, Zahir Shah in Kabul and Mohammad Reza Pahlavi in Tehran, were to leave Soviet policy makers nostalgic for earlier days. A dispassionate survey of Soviet relations with the third world in the mid-1980s might have suggested to Gorbachev and his advisers that it was in Moscow's long-run interests to increase the number of such stable capitalist interlocutors. If it was not possible to bring back the kings of Afghanistan and Iran, it might be possible, in a word, to find more Indias. This explained the great emphasis that Gorbachev laid on the right and need of different countries to pursue their own separate paths of development and on Soviet willingness to deal with them, irrespective of their social and political system.

(iv) *Third World Capitalism Re-evaluated*

Another mainstay of Marxist, and Soviet 'Marxist-Leninist' thinking on international relations and on the third world had been a theory of the inimical and retarding character of imperialism. In summary form, this view asserted that:

1. Imperialism, embodied in the ruling classes of the west, was implacably hostile to the socialist countries.

2. Imperialism exploited the third world, and thereby fostered underdevelopment.

3. The only way for third world states to develop was to break with imperialism and its world market, rely on their own productive and human resources, and develop links with the other countries of the socialist bloc.

4. The developed socialist countries too should limit their relations with the imperialist/capitalist world, and avoid being drawn into its exploitative structures.

5. The national and revolutionary movements and states in the third world can support and strengthen the Soviet bloc vis-a-vis the west.

Rethinking on some of these ideas could be seen from the mid-1970s onwards, and was encouraged by a longer-run trend in Soviet thinking, going back to the 1920s and to Varga's writings in the later 1940s, that argued against the inevitable crisis of capitalism. It was evident to all observers by the 1950s and 1960s that capitalism in the developed world was not in a terminal crisis, and with the rise of the Newly Industrializing Countries in the 1970s a similar argument began to be applied to some countries of the third world. The revisions of 'new thinking' took this process further, first with regard to capitalism in the third world, and then, with 'international *glasnost*', to a wholesale revision of the Soviet view of imperialism itself. This rethinking encompassed, therefore, not only the nature of socio-economic development in the third world, but the general nature of the US-Soviet and capitalist-socialist conflict. The five theses of the earlier viewpoint were therefore revised to read:

1. Developed capitalism is not necessarily hostile to socialism, and can, under proper conditions, compromise with it.

2. Capitalism can flourish in the third world, and may do better than a misplaced conception of socialism, for which the third world is not yet 'ready'.

3. Third world socialist states and other developing countries should participate in the world market, and benefit from the technological and trading opportunities it provides.

4. The developed socialist states should improve their links with the capitalist world, seeking a 'balance of interests' in strategy terms and mutual benefit in economic relations.

5. The third world nationalist and revolutionary movement

has nothing to contribute to the security and enhancement of the USSR, and may, through its economic demands and sharpening of international relations, actually detract from them.

Parallel to diplomatic re-consideration, therefore, there developed a corresponding re-evaluation of the socio-economic character of non-socialist third world states – in short, a more positive view of third world capitalism. The Revised Programme of the CPSU talked of 'a realistic basis for cooperation with those young states that are following the capitalist road of development'.[13] In most orthodox Soviet writing of the 1950s and 1960s the argument for socialism in the third world rested on two premises: that the transition to socialism was possible, either directly or via the non-capitalist and socialist-oriented road – and that capitalism could not achieve in the third world the goals that it proclaimed and which were necessary for these societies – independence, economic development, and political democracy. Capitalist countries in the third world were held to be under the domination of 'neo-colonialism', or, as in the case of India, to be the sites of conflict between capitalist and incipiently socialist forces.

As the difficulties of socialist transition in the third world increased, the prospects for capitalism improved: by the 1980s it was evident that capitalist states could achieve substantial rates of socio-economic development, that not all were sanguinary dictatorships, and that, if foreign policy was taken as one index of independence, they were not necessarily tied to acceptance of US foreign policy dictates. If in the early 1970s the USSR had been critical of the third world call for a New International Economic Order, on the grounds that it placed equal responsibility for the problems of the third world on the developed capitalist and socialist states, by the late 1970s it had come to endorse the NIEO and added its voice to calls for a revised international trading and financial system. The 1987 CPSU Programme explicitly endorsed the NIEO campaign. The USSR could hardly ignore the success of third world capitalism since in the 1980s it was New Industrializing Countries that did much to push Soviet exports out of western markets.

The advent of 'international *glasnost*' in 1988 coincided with a pervasive and increasingly overt crisis in many socialist and socialist-oriented states – from chronic food supply problems in Vietnam, Mozambique, Ethiopia and Nicaragua, to populist and anti-socialist insurrection in Burma and Algeria. Once this third phase had begun, Soviet writers began to compare adversely the record of third world socialist and third world capitalist régimes:

> Unfortunately, even the socialist countries of Asia encountered many difficulties in the 1960s and 1970s. Yet in the same period, contrary to what we affirmed until recently, the capitalist system in the conditions of the scientific and technological revolution turned out to have sufficient reserves. Using new instruments of expansion developed in the course of an accelerated internationalization of economic relations, namely the transnational corporation and transnational banks, it began to actively influence the social and economic development of new states. In those years a whole number of developing countries registered outwardly amazing advances on the capitalist path with the support of transnationals, forming a club of so-called new industrial states. The price paid for this and the contradictory character of the achievements was somehow ignored by the greater part of the African and Asian public. What made a strong impression was the very fact that countries had been backward shortly before became industrialized.
>
> No wonder many non-proletarian revolutionaries were disillusioned with socialist ideals. As for us, it seems to me that we were taken aback. We were unable in the period of stagnation to thoroughly revise our earlier arguments about an invariably high growth rate under socialism, the indefensibility of capitalism in new states or the existence of ample opportunities for non-capitalist development.'[16]

While the USSR was revising its view of third world capitalism and its potentialities, in their dealings with socialist-oriented states Moscow urged them to seek the bulk of their economic support elsewhere. Soviet officials impressed upon these impoverished allies the need to acquire financial support from, amongst others, Arab states that had successfully increased their bargaining position in the world oil market. Thus theoretical revision compounded diplomatic convenience, to yield a more nuanced view of capitalism in the third world as a whole and of capitalist states as potential interlocutors. The Chinese Communist Party had, of course, long since evolved a strategy based upon rallying support for as large a coalition of third world capitalist states as possible: but this was presented as a means of rallying as many 'intermediate zone' states as possible into an 'anti-hegemonic front' against the USA and the USSR, rather than as part of an overall process of reducing international tension and improving east-west ties.

Realities of Conflict

The Soviet attempt to introduce a new dynamism into nego-tiation of third world conflicts was evident in both the procla-mations of 'new thinking' and in the many diplomatic initiatives taken from 1985 onwards. In 1988, 'new thinking' developed into 'international *glasnost*', a wide-ranging and at times almost random denial of the principles on which Soviet foreign policy had hitherto been based. It was not, however, so clear that these policies would meet with success, either in the specific sense of resolving the conflicts in the countries to which they were applied, or in the broader sense of reducing east-west tension. There were more than a few substantial problems which the new Gorbachev policy would have to address, and which threatened to reduce the impact of Moscow's innovations.

The first of these concerned Soviet support for third world revolutionary movements and states. The policies of the late 1980s laid much less emphasis than hitherto on Soviet solidarity with third world revolutions, and in particular on the military role that the USSR could play in assisting such revolutions to come to power and consolidate themselves. The argument that every country had to rely on its own internal dynamics, and should choose its own path of development, served to justify a reduced Soviet commitment, as well as to warn against US or other western intervention. In his book *Perestroika* Gorbachev gave a particularly watered down definition of the communist principle of 'internationalism', as the thesis that 'no country or nation should be regarded in total separation from another, let alone pitted against another'.[17] In the section of the new edition of the CPSU Programme devoted to relations with third world states, 'internationalism' was referred to only in the context of

Soviet support for those resisting racism and apartheid. Internationalism had once meant something rather different, namely the combative solidarity of the revolutionary states of the world with all the oppressed and struggling forces in capitalist countries. It seemed, therefore, as if the USSR was retreating from its previous commitments to aid such states and movements, justifying this expediency with the argument that each state is independent and distinctive.

In fact, however, no such absolute abandonment of previous commitments was taking place, in theory or in practice. Soviet statements continued to stress support for the oppressed around the world, citing as examples Chile and South Africa, and the USSR continued to provide substantial military and economic aid to third world allies. While policies of negotiation and 'national reconciliation' were being pressed on embattled third world allies, these régimes were also concomitantly pursuing military initiatives on the battlefield, in the hope of forcing their foes onto the defensive: in Cambodia, Afghanistan, Ethiopia, Angola and Nicaragua Soviet military assistance and, in some cases, participation, was essential for the vigorous counter-insurgency campaigns pursued in 1985 and subsequent years. The Soviet forces in Afghanistan, the Vietnamese in Cambodia and the Cubans in Angola all carried out some of their most determined campaigns after Gorbachev came to power. In the economic sphere, the USSR continued to provide substantial quantities of aid to its allies: thus by 1987 around three quarters of all foreign aid to Nicaragua came from the Soviet bloc, a substantial increase on the figure for the early 1980s, and in the PDRY Soviet assistance after 1986 was being directed into a more vigorous, and apparently successful, attempt to develop that country's oil production capacity. The USSR may have been more cautious in a range of third world situations, and it did not react militarily to US assaults that were, in strategic terms, directed at Moscow – in Grenada, Lebanon and Libya. But Soviet assistance to a number of guerrilla movements – ANC, SWAPO, PLO – continued, even as Moscow sought to find negotiating opportunities for them. If one message of the 'new thinking' was that Soviet allies should be cautious, the other was that revolutionary régimes should work, and, where necessary fight, to consolidate themselves. The conflicts raging in the third world therefore allowed for less of an easy solution to the problem of reduced third world commitment than the more conciliatory exposions of 'new thinking' might have indicated.

A second difficulty with 'new thinking' was the fact that, whatever Soviet officials might say, there was no guarantee that their allies in the third world, let alone their opponents in these conflicts, would agree with them. Gorbachev had this problem in eastern Europe: while some of the ruling communist parties appeared to embrace *perestroika* enthusiastically (Hungary, Poland) others were evidently opposed, and viewed the new ideas coming from Moscow with suspicion (German Democratic Republic, Czechoslovakia, Bulgaria). In the GDR, where the régime went so far in 1988 as to ban some Soviet publications, officials argued that such things as *glasnost* were only needed in countries like the USSR which had not been through a period of bourgeois democracy: since the GDR had already passed beyond that phase, Gorbachev's innovations were unnecessary. The threat posed to party control of economy and society by Gorbachev's changes was too great for these régimes, formed in the Stalin and Brezhnev epochs, to accommodate with any enthusiasm. Similar problems emerged in the third world. In some cases, régimes introduced economic reforms that appeared to follow current Soviet thinking, but held back from any of the political changes that accompanied *perestroika* in the USSR: thus while Mongolia after the Nineteenth Party Congress in 1986 and Vietnam after the Ninth Congress in the same year lessened state control of the economy, in the hope of stimulating a private sector, the grip of their respective parties on political life remained unchanged. Only in 1988 did the MPR begin to experiment with *il tod*, the Mongolian rendering of *glasnost*. In the PDRY the party leadership reacted to the intra-party civil war of January 1986 by holding its own 'Conference', as distinct from Congress, and calling for *'alaniyya*, a rough Arabic translation of *glasnost:* but it was not evident that this had led to any substantial change in the conduct of the PDRY's political life. In Cuba, paradoxically the least orthodox of third world socialist régimes, the advent of *perestroika* in 1985 came after a number of years of experimentation with freer markets for peasant and other produce. The régime's decision to curtail this experiment and return to a more centralized system, the policy known as *rectificación*, was more than an implicit rejection of the Soviet model, since on several occasions Castro denounced the kinds of reform being introduced in the USSR as tantamount to a capitalist restoration. The Cubans, like the East Germans, liked to say that they did not need *perestroika* since they were not suffering from the same social and political problems as the USSR (see Appendix 4). With characteristic if questionable dexterity, the Cubans even claimed that they had introduced *perestroika* before the USSR. Whatever the historical record, it was evident that they, and some other third world socialist states, were more than a little uneasy about the direction in which the USSR was going.

On no issue was the divergence of the USSR and its third world allies more evident than on the issue of national reconciliation: Soviet allies were either not willing to discuss with the opposition at all, or were less than enthusiastic about the terms available. In Afghanistan, there was opposition to the whole process of 'national reconciliation' from some sections of the PDPA, and as it became evident that the USSR was going to withdraw its troops whatever the outcome there was considerable friction between the two parties. Some Afghan communists observed that if the policies of the past eight years had been mistaken, this was the fault of the USSR, since it had been running the country. The Russians replied that they were no longer prepared to sustain a régime that could not resolve its own internal differences. Ultimately, Najibullah had to accept the Soviet proposals, despite Pakistani and US refusal to cease aiding the rebels and the threat this could pose to the long-run survival of the régime, and in November 1988 over a hundred prominent PDPA members opposed to 'national reconciliation' were removed from their positions. In Ethiopia, the régime, which was not directly supported by Soviet troops, took an even more intransigent position. The Ethiopian army had been fighting guerrillas in Eritrea since 1961, for thirteen years before the revolution. While Soviet military aid had been important in permitting the Ethiopian régime to pursue its campaigns against the guerrillas, the USSR had repeatedly called for a 'political' solution and had, in contrast to other cases, itself conducted talks with representatives of the main opposition group, the Eritrean People's Liberation Front. The convening of talks with opposition forces in other allied states after 1985 did not, however, produce any change in Addis Ababa: at a press conference in May 1988 the Ethiopian leader Mengistu Haile Mariam stressed that there was no comparison between Ethiopia and the Angolan and Afghan cases. 'We have made it a point not to interfere in the internal affairs of others,' he stated. 'We expect others to behave likewise toward us'.[18] At a time when in four other Soviet allies in the third world some negotiation with guerrilla oppositions was taking place, the Ethiopian régime announced a new military offensive against the Eritreans. Mengistu did, with apparent Soviet encouragement, try to improve relations with the USA, but the Eighth Plenum of the Central Committee of the Workers' Party of Ethiopia, meeting in Addis Ababa in March 1988, proclaimed the slogan 'Everything to the War Front' as a means of confronting what it termed the 'terrorist' threat facing it.

National reconciliation, in the sense of an incorporation of previously rebel forces into a government, remained an unlikely prospect, given the degree of bitterness and rivalry that accompanies civil wars. There had, in the previous decade, been two successful cases of this, one under a revolutionary régime, the other in a counter-revolutionary: in Zimbabwe, the triumph of the ZANU–ZAPU guerrillas in 1980 was followed by the maintenance within the new state of many elements of the former white supremacist régime, including some military and intelligence personnel; in Oman, following the defeat of the PFLO guerrillas in 1975, the majority of them, including most of their leaders, crossed over to the side of the Sultan and were granted financial support and employment by his régime. Different as they were in political outcome, however, these two cases of successful 'national reconciliation' did have one common lesson: that such 'reconciliation' does not take place as a compromise, but as a result of the undisputed victory of one side. The victors allow the defeated a place in a régime that the former unequivocally control. Such a situation did not pertain to any of the cases where the USSR was urging reconciliation on its allies in the late 1980s.

The reluctance of third world allies of the Soviets to accept advice on conciliation and negotiation was by no means confined to the Afghans and the Ethiopians. In the PDRY, following the bloody feuding inside the party in January 1986, the ruling Yemen Socialist Party put on trial 138 people charged with conspiracy to stage an uprising, as a result of which nineteen were sentenced to death, including, in absentia, the former president Ali Nasir Muhammad. Great pressure was brought to bear on the YSP leaders not to proceed with the death penalties: there were public appeals from, amongst others, Yasir Arafat, Fidel Castro and Erik Honecker, and the Soviet leadership sent a special envoy, the Central Committee secretariat official Karen Brutents, with a message to the YSP leaders requesting that, in the interests of reconciliation, no death sentences should be carried out. In the end, this pressure was only partly successful: five death sentences were implemented. In the Arab-Israeli context, Soviet officials had long urged their Arab interlocutors to adopt a more concili-atory policy towards Israel, in the sense of accepting in principle the right of a separate Israeli state to exist, side-by-side with the Palestinian state the Arabs were demanding. Such advice had hitherto been implicit, or private, but in April 1988 when Arafat was in Moscow on an official visit Gorbachev publicly urged him to alter the PLO position. At the same time, Moscow was placing pressure on its most strategically important Arab ally, Syria, to modify its position on both Israel and Arafat, whose leadership of the PLO Syria had been challenging via its Palestinian client organizations since 1983.

Quite apart from areas of ethnic and factional conflict in third world states, Soviet advice aroused considerable doubts among its allies. Many doubted whether the forms of political expression associated with *glasnost* were applicable in their precarious cases. Others, not least the PDPA, argued that it was inconsistent for the USSR to criticize what they had been doing since the hither-to prevailing policies had been carried out on the instructions of Moscow itself.

Brest-Litovsk or the Nkomati Syndrome?

By far the most serious and unresolved issue underlying this new phase in Soviet foreign policy was, however, the question of how the USA and the west as a whole would react to it. There was no guarantee that the stress on interdependence and the common interests of humanity would give way to a real, effective sharing of approaches on a range of issues, involving the third world or other regions. In third world conflicts themselves, both blocs retained separate and contradictory commitments, that could only be reconciled by one prevailing over the other: in the civil war situations, one side had to win and one had to lose. This incompatibility in third world conflicts was compounded by the separate interests of regional powers – China, Pakistan, Israel, South Africa – who stood to gain in their own right from the continuation of these wars and who possessed the ability and determination to oppose any settlement that threatened their particular concerns.

The difficulties that 'new thinking' could encounter were plain enough in the case of Afghanistan. In April 1988 a set of agreements was signed in Geneva by representatives of Afghanistan, Pakistan, the USSR and the USA. These covered not only a Soviet troop withdrawal by the middle of February 1989, but also an agreement by Pakistan and Afghanistan not to interfere in each other's internal affairs or to support opposition forces in each other's territory (Appendix 3). The Soviet troop withdrawal began on schedule, on 15 May 1988, and continued thereafter: but Pakistan and the USA, far from ceasing to arm the Afghan guerrillas, maintained if not increased their arms supplies, and by the summer of 1988 there were reliable reports of Pakistani military personnel serving in Afghanistan. Faced with a defensive USSR, Islamabad and Washington systematically violated the UN agreements.

Both the USSR and the USA declared that the April 1988 agreement was important not only in itself, but also as a model of how other third world or 'regional' crises could be resolved: it soon became clear that the Soviet Union and the United States had very different understandings of what this 'importance' might be. For the USSR the agreement was a means to reduce its international military involvement and insulate a third world crisis from east-west pressures. For the USA the UN accord was an opportunity to place additional pressure on the Soviet Union and its Afghan ally and prosecute east-west rivalry with a greater prospect of success. US and other western officials claimed that in addition to the public, UN-sanctioned accord there had been a secret agreement on 'positive symmetry', under which Moscow and Washington would continue to match the arms supplies of the one to their respective clients inside Afghanistan: the USSR denied there was any such understanding, and claims by many observers that this 'positive symmetry' was contained in the texts of the UN accords themselves were unfounded, the latter expressly banning all forms of subversion and aid to opposition forces in Afghanistan and Pakistan. If the western interpretation of the UN agreement on Afghanistan was, therefore, of 'international significance', it meant that in other third world conflicts too, negotiation and ceasefire talks were regarded as a prelude to the removal from power of pro-Soviet régimes. From the response of the USA to the Geneva agreements on Afghanistan, they were important because they meant that Soviet allies should and could be replaced by pro-western forces not only in Kabul, but also in Phnom Penh, Luanda and Managua. This was hardly what Gorbachev and his advisers had intended with their 'new thinking'.

This intractable and unresolved problem pointed to the continued vitality, beneath shifting diplomatic and theoretical considerations, of the east-west conflict in the third world and more generally. Soviet 'new thinking' was an attempt to lessen the degree of western pressure in order to enable the USSR to concentrate its efforts upon internal restructuring, on *perestroika*. It was, therefore, a defensive strategy, an attempt to reduce conflict in the name of common human values and to lessen the degree of military confrontation in the third world. But it remained to be seen if, and how far, the west would accept this Soviet policy, not least because it was as plain in Washington, Tokyo, London and Paris that the USSR was in a defensive position as it was in Moscow. The response to the Afghan accords indicated that the west was quite prepared to take the offensive in such a context, with implications for other states in the third world and beyond. With the uncertainties in eastern Europe and Soviet claims that the Red Army would not intervene to crush serious oppositions, it was becoming more and more evident that new opportunities for challenging the communist parties in power, with western encouragement, were opening up. The 'reversibility' of communism was now on the agenda. In the longer run, what was at stake was the success of *perestroika*, something that Gorbachev himself repeatedly and urgently insisted was essential for the survival of the Soviet system as a whole. A setback in Afghanistan, or in other third world countries, would therefore constitute not just a defeat for 'new thinking', but would also threaten to have demonstration effects on eastern Europe and implications for the USSR itself. In seeking to insulate the USSR from the effects of third world conflict, the Soviet leadership was in other ways exposing itself to new challenges. It was aware, as were the strategic planners in Washington, that third world conflict formed part of a broader, global and politically ongoing, competition.

CONFLICT AND NEGOTIATION

A Comprehensive Logic

The argument of previous chapters has been that, following the onset of the Second Cold War in the late 1970s, there were substantial developments and changes in Soviet and US policies towards the third world. At the same time, while the third world continued to occupy an important place in the relationship between the USSR and the USA, the relative distribution of influence between the two powers shifted significantly. In the 1970s, and especially from 1974 onwards, the USA had been on the defensive in much of the third world, while the USSR had encouraged and in some respects benefited from the social and political upheavals that rocked the underdeveloped countries. This was reflected not only in Soviet actions, but also in more confident assertions of the Soviet role in world affairs. In the 1980s the USA adopted a more offensive posture. It reversed one of the fourteen revolutions of the 1970s (Grenada), challenged four others by providing military aid to their opponents (Cambodia, Afghanistan, Angola, Nicaragua), and provided increased military aid to threatened allied régimes (El Salvador, Pakistan). For its part, in the face of this strategic challenge from the USA and the urgency of the USSR's internal need for change, the USSR adopted a more cautious and conciliatory attitude. The result was that if in the 1970s it was the USA which had sought to insulate its more exposed third world commitments from challenge, and had tried, through the diplomacy of the Nixon and Carter years, to separate third world conflict from east-west relations, it was the USSR which in the 1980s was in the more vulnerable position.

As Chapters One and Two argued, third world policy forms part of a broader rivalry between east and west that derives, above all, from the contest between two distinct political and socio-economic systems. Yet this leaves many questions open. There are at least four different ways of viewing this east-west contest and the place of the third world within it. One sees the contest as, in essence, a continuation of great power conflict in the traditional sense, involving spheres of influence and the balance of power. A second approach sees Soviet–US relations in particular as a result of misperceptions, of fears and stereotypes operating on both sides to exacerbate conflict where none need exist. A third school sees inter-bloc rivalry as functional, or useful, not between the two but for the dominant powers within each bloc, the USSR and the USA. The argument here implies a fourth approach, one that sees the root of the conflict as lying in the competition of two alternative social systems. There are elements of great power rivalry in the conflict, but there is more to it than that. 'Misperception' plays its part, but leaving aside such errors of vision, there is also a conflict of interests: in this sense, the better each side knows the other, the more they may clash. There are, too, 'internal', domestic and intra-bloc, benefits to be gained from the contest, but, substantial as these are, they cannot displace or negate the importance of the overriding issues that divide each side and which fuel the competition.[1]

What is at stake, beyond bases and warheads, images and misunderstandings, is the strength and relative power of two contrasting ways of organizing societies. In this sense, a shift in one domain of the rivalry may often be explained by an increase or decrease in the resources that either side can mobilize at any one time. The ability of the USA to pursue a new, more assertive, policy in the 1980s was a reflection in the third world of a feature of the Soviet–US relationship also visible in other areas, that is, the underlying inequality in the capacities of the two sides. In the 1970s, the USSR, for all the 'stagnation' of the Brezhnev period, gave the USA a run for its money in military and third world competition. In some domains, such as that of economic performance and political liberties, the USSR was always weaker than the west: but during the 1970s it could, in some measure, offset these disadvantages by other attributes in the military and strategic fields. However, it was evident by the early 1980s that in the arms race, in third world conflicts and in the increasingly important area of economic and social competition, the USSR and its bloc were markedly and comprehensively inferior to the USA and its allies. The attack on third world revolutionary states formed, therefore, part of a much more comprehensive challenge to the USSR. It was justified not so much by the intrinsic importance of these states, but because of its contribution to over-extending the resources of the Soviet Union and undermining the ability of its allies to carry through post-revolutionary transformations. Much of the fashionable terminology of the 1980s, of 'imperial overstretch' and 'erosion of empires at the margin', was deployed to describe this approach to US–Soviet relations. The road to Moscow lay, it appeared, through Phnom Penh, Kabul, Aden, Addis Ababa, Luanda, St. Georges and Managua.

This campaign took several forms. First, US campaigns against third world revolutionary states were a good way of placing the USSR on the defensive. Aid to third world guerrillas was a function of a general exertion of western power against the USSR, and a desire to stretch its resources to breaking point. Second, the pressure in the third world had, as its goal, not only the weakening of these states themselves, but the overall credibility of the Soviet system and of Soviet power. The use of armed forces without fear of riposte – in Lebanon, Libya, Grenada – while strategically insignificant did serve to underline the relative weakness of the USSR. The prospect of overwhelming the PDPA in Afghanistan was important not only for that country, but also for the demonstration effect of such a Soviet setback on eastern Europe and, it was anticipated, within the multi-ethnic USSR itself.

The Reagan Years: Alternative Balance-Sheets

This competitive and comprehensive view of US–Soviet relations in the third world led some supporters of US policy to claim that, in broad terms, Reagan's strategy had been a success. Thus while he was running for re-election in 1984 Reagan was fond of saying that since acceding to office there had been no revolutionary victories in the third world. Writing in mid-1988 John Whitehead, a deputy secretary of state in the Reagan Administration, laid out what he saw as the seven 'achievements' of the Reagan era:

1. Relations with the Soviets are good and continue to improve.
2. The Soviets are getting out of Afghanistan.
3. The Vietnamese are starting to take their troops out of Cambodia.
4. There is a plan to get Cuban troops out of Angola.
5. We are moving closer to an end of the Iran–Iraq war.
6. Freedom and democracy are on the move all over the world.
7. Free economic systems are prospering.[2]

While accurate enough in portraying the strategic intention of US policy, this balance-sheet invited contradiction in a number of respects. It portrayed in dubiously euphemistic light processes that had profoundly negative consequences for many people in the world, such as the ravages of world recession in the 1980s: even in the EEC, one in eight persons was living at or below the poverty level. Point 6 claimed credit for processes to which the USA had either been indifferent, or had indeed sought until the last moment to block: it constituted an ambitious, if implausible, attempt to obliterate US responsibility for the dictatorships that had endured in these states and simultaneously to claim credit for opposition advances in such countries as South Korea, the Philippines, Pakistan and Chile. Even where there had been a US policy change before the régime in question was challenged directly, this shift had not occurred in state policy: whatever contribution the US had made to resisting apartheid in South Africa, this had come more from the Congress, with its advocacy of sanctions, than from the executive branch itself.

There were, however, rather more profound reasons why this apparently plausible balance-sheet needed some critical examination. First, for all the claims made for Reagan's policy, the Republican administration had in all its eight years failed to conclude a single significant diplomatic success resolving a conflict in the third world, nothing compared to Nixon and Kissinger's achievement in China and Carter's in the Arab-Israeli dispute. The agenda of third world problems on which the USA had a special influence remained unchanged in January

1989 from a decade before: Israel was in the grip of the Palestinian *intifadha*, there had been no movement on Israel's side towards realizing the second part of the Camp David accords, on Palestinian independence, and the Israeli elections of November 1988 strengthened the hand of those opposed to a settlement; in South Africa, the white régime was holding on, after making some token concessions, and was ceding ground to the extreme nationalist right; in Chile, Pinochet remained defiant. In these crucial areas involving states allied to Washington, which had been evident areas of concern to US policy when Reagan took office, the record of the Reagan years was one of stalemate, evasion and potential or actual explosion.

The record where the USA *had* acted was equally debatable. Whitehead claimed that the US should take credit for progress on ending the Iran-Iraq war; within days of his article being published Iran did accept a ceasefire, accepting UN Security Council Resolution 598 of July 1987. But the US role in this, both through military deployment in the Gulf and through the framing of a western and UN policy that was tilted against Iran had, if anything, served to prolong the war for months and years longer than might otherwise have been the case. Secondly, the very military activism of Reagan in the third world had produced the two greatest crises of his administration, in the Lebanon debacle of 1982–1984 and the Irangate scandal of 1986–1987. For all that Reagan was able to control these, they placed his administration on the defensive in a way that highlighted the weakness of the military approach and confirmed the reluctance of the US public, despite its affection for Reagan himself, to get directly involved in third world conflicts: the Vietnam Syndrome was as strong in 1988 as it was in 1978, while in Congress the reaction to both crises was to strengthen legislative control over direct and covert operations in the third world. Reagan's third world policies also contributed to increasing strains between the USA and its allies: over Grenada in 1983, and Libya in 1986. Both made it more difficult for European governments to endorse US policy as a whole, and the latter drew unwelcome attention to the ease with which NATO facilities could be used for 'out of area' operations.

Most important of all, however, the new more forward US posture did not lead to the ignominious retreat by the USSR that the originators of the strategy had anticipated. If the USSR was more cautious and open to negotiations, it nonetheless continued to meet many of its commitments to third world allies under siege. In 1986–1988 all of the Soviet allies facing military challenge from US-backed forces were able, with Soviet backing, to launch offensives against the forces confronting them. In Ethiopia and Afghanistan these did not meet with success, and in the latter in particular the régime remained under serious threat. But elsewhere the rebel forces were hard hit: in Angola, where the MPLA, backed by a strengthened Cuban support force, hit hard at UNITA in the middle of 1988; in Nicaragua, where the *contras* remained on the defensive and were forced to sue for peace in June 1988, after withdrawing much of their combat strength to Honduras; in Cambodia, where the Vietnamese drove some of the rebel forces towards the Thai frontier, and provoked an open division in their ranks. On the economic front, the USSR was less able to provide what these régimes required: but here too many long-standing commitments continued to be met, even if Soviet officials were now more honest about shortcomings within these countries. In the case of Nicaragua, at least, US pressure led to a substantial increase in Soviet economic support as noted above: by 1988 around 75% of all economic aid to the FSLN government was coming from the Soviet bloc. The USSR was placed under greater strain; it did not, however, simply retreat.

Soviet–US Negotiation: Regional Issues

It was in this context of often ferocious rivalry between the USA and the USSR across three continents that another dimension of their relations now acquired greater prominence, namely that of bilateral negotiations on 'regional issues'. In themselves, such bilateral discussions and negotiations on third world crises were not entirely new and a number of such negotiations and understandings had been reached at various points in the post-1945 period. There had been semi-explicit understandings on controlling the extent of combat even during the Korean and Vietnam wars; in 1962 Moscow and Washington had co-sponsored the neutralization of Laos; in both the 1967 and 1973 Arab-Israeli wars they had worked together, through the UN Security Council, to contain the fighting and introduce cease-fires; in 1977–1978 they had reached an unannounced but explicit understanding on controlling the fighting in the Horn of Africa, between Ethiopia and Somalia. These partial understandings had, however, been limited in scope, designed to resolve specific and often dangerous crises, rather than to build longer-term collaboration between the two.

From 1985 onwards, however, bilateral negotiation took a new form. Regular meetings of officials to discuss third world questions were taking place in early 1985; after Gorbachev came to power and expounded his new ideas at the April 1985 Plenum of the CPSU Central Committee, such talks, between Soviet Foreign Ministry and State Department officials, and deputy foreign ministers and assistant secretaries of state, acquired a more noticeable momentum and substance. There were regular, as distinct from crisis-related, meetings between officials on both sides to discuss regional issues; these questions were routinely included on the agenda when experts and relevant officials talked at Soviet–US summits; and through contacts and in some cases pressure on their respective allies in the third world, both sides sought to find answers to major international problems. The exact content of such negotiations was not publicized and rarely leaked, and even the fact of their occurrence, and the place of meeting, was frequently not publicly announced. Both US and Soviet officials insisted that no actual negotiation took place at these meetings, but rather that both sides used them to explore and make negotiating positions more precise, and to issue un-official warnings to the other, on arms supplies, for example, or suspicious naval deployments. Thus US officials used such talks to warn of Soviet arms shipments to Nicaragua, Soviet officials to emphasize their commitment to Syria. Many of the major multilateral negotiations – on Afghanistan, the Persian Gulf, the Arab-Israeli dispute, southern Africa, Central America – were supplemented and in some measure impelled forward by such discreet Soviet–US exchanges.

A brief overview of diplomatic activity in 1987 and 1988 can illustrate just how far this stimulation of negotiation in third world crisis situations had gone:

1. Korean peninsula: intermittent talks between the DPRK and ROK, with considerable Soviet and Chinese pressure on the DPRK to continue negotiation.

2. Indo-China: direct talks between Cambodia prime minister Hu Sen and opposition coalition leader Norodom Sihanouk, with Soviet encouragement to both Cambodia and Vietnam to find a settlement, and Vietnamese and Soviet discussions with ASEAN states, particularly Thailand; Soviet encouragement of direct Sino-Vietnamese talks, and deputy ministerial talks between the USSR and China on a settlement, as a prelude to a Sino-Soviet summit in 1989, the first in thirty years.

3. Afghanistan: UN-sponsored talks involving Afghanistan, Pakistan, the USSR and the USA led to signing of Geneva accords on 20 April 1988, under which all Soviet combat forces left Afghanistan by 15 February 1989.

4. Gulf war: after several unsuccessful mediation attempts by the UN, the Non-Aligned Movement, the Islamic League, Sweden and Algeria, Iran accepted UN Security Council 598 of 20 July 1987 and on 20 August 1988 a cease-fire between the two came into operation.

5. Arab–Israeli dispute: after years of paralysis, the USA and the USSR moved somewhat closer to agreeing on the terms of an international conference, while the USSR re-established contact with Israel and publicly encouraged the PLO to accept Israel's right to exist. In December 1988 Arafat stated clearly that the PLO was willing to negotiate with Israel and to accept a two-state solution, while within Israel itself a significant minority favoured negotiations with Arab states.

6. Cyprus: despite the failure of earlier attempts by UN Secretary-General Perez de Cuellar to reconcile the Greek Cypriot and Turkish Cypriot positions, prospects improved following the election as president of Georgi Vassiliou and direct meetings between Greek premier Papandreou and Turkish premier Ozal.

7. Chad: following years of conflict between Libya and Chad, in which the USSR and France supported their respective allies, and during which Libya occupied part of northern Chad and supported the Chadian opposition forces, the two countries reached agreement on 3 October 1988 on a peaceful settlement of disputes.

8. Horn of Africa: the animosity between Somalia and Ethiopia, sustained through public propaganda and mutual support for each other's dissidents after the 1977–1978 war between them, gave way in 1987 to a substantial agreement

between them on reducing tension and non-interference. Prior to this accord, the Cuban forces in Ethiopia, which had been stationed along the frontier with Somalia, were gradually reduced in an unannounced process that brought the total from over 10,000 in the early 1980s to a few hundred in 1988.

9. Angola: in April 1988, with US and Soviet encouragement, four-party talks to resolve the Angolan dispute began between representatives of the MPLA government in Angola, Cuba, South Africa and the USA. A cease-fire between Cuban and South African troops came into operation in Angola on 22 August and in December a composite agreement was reached: this covered not only Cuban and South African troop withdrawals from Angola, but also a procedure by which these troop withdrawals could be linked to the independence of Namibia, under South African occupation since 1915.

10. Western Sahara: on 30 August 1988 an agreement was reached under UN auspices for a settlement of the war taking place there between Moroccan forces, which had occupied the area upon the Spanish departure in 1975, and POLISARIO, the guerrilla force backed by Algeria. Under this agreement a referendum would be held in Western Sahara to decide whether or not it remained part of Morocco.

11. Central America: in 1987 Costa Rican President Arias organized a conference of the five Central American states to achieve a settlement of the several wars being prosecuted in the area, most notably those in Nicaragua and El Salvador. Talks between the FSLN government in Managua and representatives of the *contras* began in 1986 and, despite substantial disagreements, led to a cease-fire in June 1988.

In historical perspective, this spate of negotiations represented an unprecedented attempt to deal with the legacies of several waves of international conflict. In the majority of cases, it involved grappling with the legacy of the late 1970s and with the agenda, across three continents, that the upheavals of that period had generated. These had provided much of the tinder for Cold War II; Indo-China, Afghanistan, the Persian Gulf, the Horn of Africa, Angola, Mozambique, Western Sahara, Nicaragua. In part, the coincidence was a product of exhaustion: the forces involved here had come to realize that military conflict alone could not resolve the issues, and that some compromise and exploration of political breathing-space was needed. Equally, they were encouraged by changes in the policies of their international supporters – in most cases this included the USA and the USSR, and these great powers in turn promoted greater flexibility from the interested regional powers. If it was true of changes in Israel, South Africa, Algeria–Morocco amongst others, it was above all the case for a major regional actor long practised at using Soviet–US rivalry for its own ends – the People's Republic of China: abandoning the partisanship with the USA which had characterized so much of its policies in the Far East and the third world more generally throughout the 1970s leading it to support the 1973 coup in Chile, to arm UNITA, and to go to war with Vietnam, Peking in the 1980s adopted a more independent and balanced position that enabled it to play, in some situations, a less provocative role.

This prompting by the great powers, and the wider feeling that old commitments and paralyses could not be sustained for ever had, however, an impact on conflicts that predated the late 1970s and which had remained in various forms of limbo over the decades: in the Korean Peninsula, the Arab-Israeli dispute, and southern Africa. The spate of negotiations did not represent a simple, shared, determination, nor was it a product of mere coincidence: it reflected a new international conjuncture, and varying layers of international pressure, from the UN, through the USSR and the USA, down to regional states upon the conflicts in question.

A Mosaic of Intractables

This panorama of negotiation and apparent willingness to compromise was not, of course, as complete as many would have wished. There were more than a few conflicts, within and between states, where no progress was being registered in the late 1980s: in Timor, where the Indonesian forces that had occupied this former Portuguese colony in 1975 were still battling the FRETILIN guerrillas; in Eritrea and southern Sudan where guerrilla forces fighting Ethiopia and the Sudan respectively, and backed by the rival states, were plunging the region into protracted misery compounded by famine and appalling climatic conditions – in the Sudan, the Islamic right were blocking compromise with the non-Islamic south, while in Ethiopia, the régime was resisting international, including Soviet, pressure to find a compromise in Eritrea; in Lebanon, where the initial hopes after the Israeli and Palestinian withdrawals of 1982–4 had given way to new divisions between and within the Christian and Muslim communities and where, in September 1988, a sort of de facto partition came about, with the régime of General Aoun in the Christian east of Beirut, and that of premier Salim al-Huss in the west; in Mozambique where, despite hopes raised by the Maputo–Pretoria Nkomati agreement in 1984 guerrillas of RENAMO, backed by South Africa, continued to take a terrible toll on population and economy; in Peru, where the guerrillas of *Sendero Luminoso*, ferociously organized and inspired by a residual Maoism, were able to gain significant ground amidst conditions of great economic hardship.

Nor were intractable and perennial wars an exclusive prerogative of the third world: in Europe some of the most long-standing of civil and national conflicts had acquired a new virulence and seemed especially impermeable to resolution – in Ireland, the Basque country, and Kosovo. Indeed the strength of ethnic and communal conflicts in Europe, and not least their smouldering extension in eastern Europe, suggested that this question above all, the spread and growth of ethnic conflicts in new social and political situations might be the preoccupying concern of the future. If Ireland showed the way, the Philippines and Sri Lanka, Punjab and Lebanon, Burundi and Assam followed suit. Far from being relics of earlier times, these conflicts, for all the 'avatism' invoked, were products of new social and political situations that resulted from political independence and social change: the recipe for such conflicts, across much of the developed and developing world, was immense. As Ireland, Cyprus and the Arab-Israeli dispute showed, these conflicts were the most intractable of all: inter-state conflicts might be settled by compromise, revolutionary and social contests had, in the end, an outcome one way or the other. Ethnic and communal violence, drawing on a selective and unnegotiable invocation of 'history' and souring relations between groups doomed to live in the same area, permitted no such amelioration.

Beyond these intractable issues, however, there lay wider international factors that put a question mark over the possibility of resolution in the crises under negotiation, and which suggested that, even if there was some kind of success in one or two of them, these local and regional initiatives would be transformed into a broader transformation of the east-west conflict in the third world. In the first place, there were many participants in these regional conflicts who stood to lose by a process of negotiation, at least by one carried out under the terms prevailing in the late 1980s: they, and their regional backers, were liable to have reduced influence in settlements where the currently stronger party remained in a position of dominance. Whatever the persuasive and other influences of the USA and the USSR over these third world allies, there was little likelihood that they could simply coerce them into accepting solutions detrimental to them. As so often in post-1945 developments, the catalyst for east-west conflict lay as much in the contradictions of the third world as in the dynamics of Soviet–US rivalry itself. If this was true of the USA vis-a-vis Israel or South Africa, it was equally true for the USSR vis-a-vis the DPRK or Cambodia, let alone the PDPA.

This consideration, of the resistance of local allies, would be quite consistent with a situation in which the great powers themselves were seeking to find lasting compromises in third world situations. But this too was a presumption which, albeit much repeated in official statements and editorials of the late 1980s, was open to doubt. On the Soviet side, there remained, muted and reduced as it was, and with all the new benevolence towards 'imperialism', a commitment to supporting established revolutionary régimes in the third world and to supporting revolutionary forces in a number of countries, including Palestine, South Africa, Namibia and El Salvador. The USSR had not simply abdicated the commitments enunciated in the 1950s and 1960s. On the US side, there was an even more overt commitment to altering the existing situation in the third world, evident in the Reagan Doctrine and its associated neo-interventionist policies. For its part, US policy aimed not only to prevent the triumph of revolutionary régimes, by assisting established régimes to crush opponents and by influencing political crises in allied states, but also to use a combination of 'pro-insurgency' policies against third world revolutionary régimes and diplomatic pressures to put the USSR and its allies on the defensive.

The very fact of negotiation is rarely, in itself, an indication that conflicts previously expressed in a wholly military form have ended or lost their dynamic: negotiation, especially in a situation where there is no cease-fire, can equally be seen as an instrument for compounding initiatives on the ground with political manoeuvre. Classic examples of this in the post-1945 period have included the 1954 Geneva conference in Indo-China, during the very course of which the Vietminh clinched victory by destroying the French expeditionary base at Dien Bien Phu; the 1968–1973 US–Vietnamese negotiations in Paris, which led, following substantial Vietnamese pressure, to a US troop withdrawal in 1973; and the 1980 Lancaster House negotiations on the independence of Zimbabwe, where the entry of the ZANU–ZAPU guerrillas into state power in Harare was only guaranteed by their simultaneous campaigns on the ground against the Smith régime.

In situations of inter-state war, negotiation can introduce compromise and be a prelude to some mutually acceptable resolution especially when accompanied by cease-fire. In situations of internal social conflict, when one party is out of state power and the other holds it, such shared benefits are far harder to arrive at, and negotiations, far from paving the way for a compromise, may well be the means by which one party, assisted by international forces favouring a settlement, consolidates its predominance over the other. Many third world conflicts involve an element of both – an internal conflict, along social and/or ethnic lines, with external forces involved on the other side. Solutions in such situations follow the different logics of the case: the conflicting states may well resolve their dispute, but at the expense of one or other of the internally conflicting forces. Those out of power, once they lose the backing of an external state, have to accept the situation: both international and internal pressures conspire to block their resistance to an established state.

Such a prospect gives Soviet–US negotiations on the third world a particular meaning, in which one or other concedes ground in a specific third world situation, at the expense of a local ally – the PDPA in Afghanistan, for the USSR, the *contras* in Nicaragua or UNITA in Angola for the USA. Beyond the

148

formality of compromise and negotiation, there lies a continuity of pressure and rivalry that is combined with the attempt to reduce direct Soviet–US confrontation in third world situations. The spate of negotiations of the late 1980s certainly represented a change in many conflicts, and in Soviet–US relations as a whole: but it did not represent an end to the competition between east and west, or their commitment to sustaining allies and challenging foes in the third world as a whole.

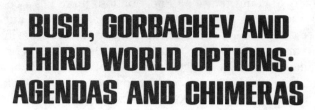

BUSH, GORBACHEV AND THIRD WORLD OPTIONS: AGENDAS AND CHIMERAS

1988: Interlude or Turning-point?

In 1988, both major powers underwent important changes in political leadership. In September Gorbachev was installed in the USSR as President, after three years of increasing power as General Secretary, and in November George Bush was elected as President of the USA, after eight years as Vice-President. A new and potentially more pacific phase in east-west diplomatic relations had begun, building on the advances of the immediately preceding negotiations. These twin elections, marking a new phase of executive leadership within an overall continuity, had implications for third world policy as well as for other major elements of the Soviet–US relationship. The conjuncture of the late 1980s therefore appeared to mark a moment at which substantial re-thinking and reformulation of policy towards the third world is in the offing. Parallel to presidential elections in the USA and the USSR, the latter part of 1988 in particular represented a turning point. The ebb and flow of conflict and negotiation in the third world during the previous decade had produced international negotiations and compromises over a dozen or so questions. Now Soviet forces were withdrawing from Afghanistan, cease-fires were agreed upon in Nicaragua, Angola and the Iran–Iraq war, substantive negotiations began on Western Sahara and Cambodia, and there was even some movement on two of the toughest chestnuts, the Arab-Israeli dispute and the Korean Peninsula.

Both sides openly recognized the degree to which resolution

of third world questions was of global, rather than of merely national or regional importance. The evolution and implementation of policy towards the third world had preoccupied both the USA and the USSR since they emerged as the constituents of the bipolar world in 1945, and had accounted for some of their greatest successes as well as failures. Problems arose not only in dealing with political forces in the third world, but also within the society and state apparatus of these two leading states themselves: one of the reasons for Khrushchev's downfall in 1964 was his mishandling of the Cuban missile crisis. As the authors of *Discriminate Deterrence* amongst others had emphasized, third world issues had undermined the position of numerous post-war American presidents. On not a few occasions, the USA and the USSR had found the third world creating difficulties in relations with their respective allies. The friction between the USA on the one hand and France and Britain on the other, and between the USSR and China is evidence enough of this.

Dogmatism of the Benign: The Advent of 'International *Glasnost*'

On the Soviet side, the perception of third world issues was different to that in the USA, but equally pressing. By the latter half of 1988 there had been substantial evolution in content and style beyond the initial 'new thinking' positions staked out by Gorbachev in 1985 and 1986. Apart from its pieties about Western policy, 'international *glasnost*' involved a wide-ranging rejection of previous Soviet commitments, and a denial of the third world's role in advancing socialism. In the Soviet view, the third world constituted a domain of instability and crises where there was a risk of great-power confrontation. Even if it fell short of confrontation, the involvement of the great powers presented special dangers for peace and for a reduction of east-west tension. In the context of Gorbachev's 'new thinking', the cost of third world involvement was not just economic or military, but also an international or global one. What was most important was that such involvements, by undermining Soviet–US understandings, inhibited the concentration of ener-

gies and resources on domestic Soviet concerns. In contrast
to the classical Marxist-Leninist view that the development of
socialism in the USSR would be enhanced by increased revolutionary struggle and socialist commitment in the colonial and
third worlds, 'new thinking' implied, as discussed in Chapter
four, that in order to consolidate and transform the USSR it was
necessary to limit the extent of this struggle and of Soviet
commitment and involvement in it. Soviet writers now flatly
denied that national liberation movements were beneficial to
the USSR. Marxist theory apart, 'new thinking' was able to
play on a widespread sense of disillusion and hostility within
the USSR towards third world socialist allies. They were blamed,
with varying degrees of justice, for economic shortages and for
poor relations with the USA. Emphasis upon 'national interest'
and on nationalism therefore served to turn this Soviet isola-
tionism to the cause of *perestroika*. The old concept of
'correlation of forces' was replaced by a new 'balance of
interests', something supposedly acceptable to east and west.

By the time Gorbachev was elected President of the USSR
in October 1988 the introductory ideas of 1985 had been taken
much further. On the one hand, 1988 had become the year not
just of Soviet statements, but of Soviet agreement to a set of
regional agreements in which their influence and prestige was
at stake: most prominently Afghanistan, but also the Gulf and
Angola. Alongside these specific agreements, and the INF treaty
with the USA, there began the process of 'international *glasnost* '
as discussion opened up on foreign policy within the USSR. If in
the first three years of *glasnost* more open discussion had been
confined to a range of domestic issues, this restriction did not
hold in 1988, when, with evident support from the top, a range of
criticisms and new ideas were voiced. Thus Foreign Minister
Shevardnadze pioneered the theme that 'national interest' as
distinct from internationalist class solidarity should determine,
and by implication limit Soviet foreign involvements, whilst a
senior official of his Ministry openly criticized the idea that there
was anything within the US political system implicitly hostile
to the USSR. As the months passed, it became more and more
possible for Soviet officials to question their previous involvements in the third world, and to doubt the socialist credentials
of third world allies.[2]

Western Policy in the Third World: Four Options

US foreign policy and official pronouncements in the early 1980s had been dominated by a Soviet 'threat' and the relation of third world upheaval to it. In the discussion of the late 1980s, by contrast, there was increasing recognition in some quarters that third world issues could be separated from Soviet–US relations, and that it was third world conflict as linked to Soviet–US relations, as much as the nuclear arms race, that undermined east-west negotiation and threatened the interests of the USA. Thus if hitherto the threat from the third world had been presented as a composite Soviet-revolutionary one, the Soviet role was now often reduced in proportion, and the revolutionary threat was linked to other threats to the USA, especially those of Islamic fundamentalism, terrorism and narcotics. Third world debt, especially in its Latin American variant, was increasingly seen as a greater menace to the stability of the USA than revolution. This uncoupling from the 'Soviet' threat gave the third world a minatory dimension more distinct and cogent than it had ever possessed before. A new inter-ventionism, unconnected with rivalry with the USSR, thereby became feasible.

Assessment of America's changing attitudes to the third world, and of the options facing Bush, was made the more difficult by the apparently small place of third world issues, and indeed international issues as a whole, in the 1988 US election. None of the rival campaigns focussed on this, and surveys of voters indicated that they too placed little emphasis upon international issues in making their choice. This contrasted strikingly with the 1980 election, when the Soviet 'menace' and its third world extensions, and of course Iran, had been so prominent. Yet this apparent neglect belied the reality: the new US attitude towards the third world was a permissive condition for the apparently anodyne exercise in mediatic democracy that brought George Bush to the White House. The changes in Soviet policy had enabled US politicians to concentrate almost exclusively on domestic issues, and, over the preceding eight years, Reagan had re-formed a bipartisan approach to the third world which neither Irangate nor the persistence of the 'Vietnam Syndrome' could override. If Reagan's policy had avoided direct commitments of US troops, in the Vietnam manner, and had been battered by Irangate, it nonetheless advocated the necessity and legitimacy of US intervention in third world crises by other means. These included 'preventive diplomacy': the management of revolutionary crises, 'pro-insurgency', the support for counter-revolutionary forces, and increased military assistance to US allies. As a former director of the CIA, Bush himself could be expected to endorse a range of covert actions in the third world: while the cause of the *contras* appeared to be in demise, two of the policies that Bush seemed committed to from the beginning were increased military aid to El Salvador and continued support for UNITA. If Bush therefore inherited an America that was less anxious about international issues, and in particular about the USSR, the new consensus in the USA favoured a measured interventionism in the world.[1] Not surprisingly, there were those in Washington who argued that, by reaching agreement with Moscow, Washington would have a freer hand to intervene in the third world.

The shifts in the international context provoked considerable debate within the western foreign policy community, both official and unofficial. With new Soviet thinking on the third world, and some Soviet–US rapprochement, it became possible to discern at least four broad strains of thought in the US discussion of how to formulate third world policy. The first of these, already discussed in Chapter Five, was that of a joint US–Soviet approach to specific third world crises. This could be categorized generally as the option of 'condominium'. Earlier versions had included the 1972 Basic Principles Agreement and the 1977 Vance-Gromyko statement on the Middle East, as well as, in an even earlier epoch, the 1945 Charter of the UN itself. The Charter gave special roles, diplomatic and coercive, including that of joint military action, to the five great powers of that epoch.

As already indicated, the idea prevalent in the late 1980s of a joint Soviet–US policy on third world issues faced two, equally insurmountable, obstacles: first, the persistence of socio-economic competition, and the inability of the great powers themselves to find sufficient trust and agreement to put a joint policy into effect; second, the resistance of third parties, including states and revolutionary movements in the third world, to solutions imposed from outside. Since such third world forces had prior commitments from the great powers they had considerable scope for initiatives that would disrupt great power discussions and bring their allies in on their side of the conflict. The lesson of post-1945 history was, if anything, that it was precisely at moments of great power rapprochement that the junior allies of both sides became more restive; China broke with the USSR at the time of the US–Soviet thaw of the late 1950s and early 1960s, and both Israel and Egypt were quick to oppose the 1977 US–Soviet agreement on the Middle East.

The second option can be subsumed under the term 'interdependence', a concept that became fashionable in academic and official analysis of international relations during the 1970s. This term suggested that old-style military competition between states was increasingly being replaced by economic, ideological and social interaction and that the growth of these non-military ties would reduce the risks of military confrontation. The term was originally applied to relations between developed capitalist countries of the OECD to stress their growing economic interpenetration and hence the lessening possibility of conflict between them. The likelihood of war between the USA and Canada, or between different EEC countries, had certainly vanished in the postwar epoch. The term was, however, extended to cover relations between developed capitalist and third world countries, as in the two Brandt Reports of 1980 and 1983, and, by further extension, to cover relations between the western and Soviet blocs. At times, 'interdependence' was used to refer not to the economic interrelationship of broadly similar countries, but to the military balance between the two blocs themselves, with the implication that deterrence and the disposal of nuclear forces on both sides precluded military conflict. At other times, and this was especially true in the Soviet usage of the term as part of 'new thinking', interdependence was used to suggest that if east and west could maximize their economic interrelationships by official agreements this would minimize the danger of military conflict. In the late 1980s it appeared that, beyond direct economic advantages, the USSR was encouraging western investment and trade in the USSR not just for direct economic advantage but in the hope that this would lessen the danger of war in the future[3].

The term 'interdependence' is ambivalent, both illuminating

and confused. If it identifies a real process in the contemporary world, it also mixes up the reality of growing interconnection with a wish that this interconnection will increase global harmony, and with an often unfounded belief that this process has reduced the power of states. In fact, alongside growing interdependence, there have arisen new conflicts in the world, and states, while losing control in some areas, have gained it in others. The ironic result of this confused appeal was that in the 1970s interdependence became one of the key concepts of the Trilateral Commission, the private body responsible for much of the policy of the Carter Administration, and a decade later, it became a corner-stone of Soviet 'new thinking'. In both cases 'interdependence' involved the belief that old style confrontation was dying out, and that economic links were creating a more flexible and peaceful world, in which conflicts of the old kind would disappear or at least be more manageable.

The idea that economic links reduce military confrontation, apparently in conformity with common sense, is an old one, running through much eighteenth and nineteenth century liberal thought. Yet it is far less solid a basis for policy than might seem to be the case, since it overstates the degree to which issues of strategic and political conflict can be submerged by economic ties. It received a sharp rebuff with the outbreak of World War I, which threw into total war states that had been trading and investing actively with each other. Similarly, if in less destructive form, Carter's belief in the beneficent effects of trade was followed by the onset of Cold War II, when economic relations between east and west became themselves an object of strategic manipulation. Far from using it for beneficent means, the USA sought to impose restrictions on trade with the USSR and hence to weaken it by such embargoes as well as to force Moscow into an arms race that it could afford even less than the USA. In describing relations between developed countries of similar socio-political complexion, the term 'interdependence' has considerable validity, even though here too it may understate the degree of protectionism and competition involved in such interaction. On the other hand, in providing a basis for north-south relations or east-west ones, it assumes that in the end economic benefit will prevail over strategic interest, something that has, in the past at least, very often proved not to be the case. A third world policy that rests upon the prospect of 'interdependence' runs the risk of that of the liberal internationalists prior to 1914 and of the Trilateralists in the 1970s. It would be naive to presume that increased interdependence between the Soviet and western economic systems will of itself resolve problems.

The third option, favoured by many American liberals and now adopted by some Soviet exponents, is that of 'nonintervention' and 'demilitarization' of both Soviet and US relations with the third world. In the face of Vietnam, and of subsequent attempts to revive a commitment to military involvement in the third world, US liberals have argued the case for the US keeping out of such involvements: the cost is too high, the third world states and issues do not really matter. In essence, America can afford to ignore these crises, and should cease exaggerating their strategic importance, and the degree of Soviet involvement in them. Moreover, these liberal critics argue, military intervention does not work: Vietnam and Afghanistan are cases in point. A clear statement of this view was given by a joint report produced in 1988 by the American Committee on US–Soviet Relations and the USA–Canada Institute of the Academy of Sciences of the USSR. In addition to discussing nuclear issues, the two sides surveyed the past pattern of US–Soviet involvement in the third world, and in a gesture of even-handedness, listed the examples of such activity by either side. It then stated:

> The proposal to demilitarize US–Soviet competition in the third world has far-reaching implications. To be effective it would have to include agreement (1) not to intervene directly or indirectly with military force; (2) not to transfer a specified list of sophisticated weapons, together with a mutual understanding to influence other major arms suppliers to adopt the same policy; (3) not to introduce proxy military forces or volunteer forces or covert paramilitary forces into regional conflicts; (4) not to organize, fund, equip or advise insurgencies or counter-insurgencies; (5) to limit military assistance programs to equipment and training necessary only for legitimate defense; (6) to offer military protection to friends and allies only against a cross-border invasion; (7) and to

establish machinery to insure adequate verification of these agreements.[4]

This list of implications of non-intervention and demilitarization spelled out in clearer terms many of the issues raised in the 1972 Basic Principles agreement; by the same token, it ran the risk of foundering for many of the same reasons that had undermined the earlier declaration. First, the list of implications itself and the preceding historical survey of Soviet and US interventions in the third world betrayed some polemical simplification: a number of points were accepted by each side in the context of the joint study, but such bipolar bonhomie could not, in itself, assure the accuracy of the account provided. For example, the use by the joint US–Soviet report of the term 'proxy', frequently summoned up by US writers to refer to the Cuban forces in Angola and Ethiopia, ignored the degree to which Cuba acted of its own volition, however much this accorded with Soviet policy as a whole, and the fact that in both these countries Cuba was defending an established, and internationally recognized state against attack from outside. In the list of third world military interventions for which the report criticized the USSR was included South Yemen in 1978: a minor detail, perhaps, this, were it not for the fact that no such intervention occurred.[5] A policy based upon the exchanging of token myths and on repeating the baneful and inaccurate litany of the US right, could hardly form a secure basis for greater international understanding.

History apart, there were other problems with this proposal for a demilitarized régime. In terms all too reminiscent of the League of Nations and its utopian approach to international relations, this liberal blueprint for the 1980s ignored key questions that underlie international tension. Thus in pointing to Vietnam and Afghanistan it tried to confirm the proposition that military intervention should be rejected because it does not work. An equally cogent case could, however, be made for the counter-proposition: the reason why military intervention, direct and indirect, remains attractive in international affairs, is that in many cases it has worked, as the list of Soviet and US interventions since 1945 makes clear – in Hungary and Czechoslovakia as much as in the Dominican Republic and Grenada. As with torture, the case against intervention is rendered less, not more, effective if it rests upon the claim that it does not work. The bitter truth is that it does work often enough, and the threat of it therefore works more often still, for it to be an effective and therefore all the more disturbing feature of international relations: the US interventions in the Dominican Republic in 1965 and in Grenada in 1983 were evidence enough of that.

The impracticality of the 1988 report's liberal non-intervention position was also evident in the way it excluded direct military assistance even when states were attacked from outside – leaving it unclear how, in the face of this not infrequent feature of international relations, third world states were supposed to respond. Moreover, it failed to resolve the conundrum which non-intervention poses for liberal analysis: the report implied that existing governments the world over were to be regarded as legitimate, and that no opposition forces were to be backed with military means against established régimes, even if these were oppressive and undemocratic. This bipolar understanding would, therefore, freeze unjust social and political orders in many states, preventing the establishment of more just arrangements because this would discomfit Washington and Moscow. The logic of non-intervention, liberal in its origins, thereby encouraged the institutionalization of repression.

A New Interventionism

The first three policy orientations – condominium, interdependence and non-intervention – rested upon some degree of US–Soviet understanding and a continuation and enhancement of the negotiations under way from 1986 onwards. Parallel to these, however, there lay a fourth option, represented by the return of a belief in unilateral intervention in the third world. Though this had been evident in the USSR in the late 1970s, as demonstrated by the intervention in Afghanistan in December 1979, it was in the US discussion of the 1980s that the revival of interventionism was most clear. In the face of any defeat, there can be two reactions: either intervention should not be attempted again or it *should* be tried again, but done better. If the liberal policy of non-intervention represented one US response to Vietnam, there was another strain, which sought to re-enact

159

third world intervention, but on the basis of the 'lessons' of the Vietnam war.

As discussed in Chapter 3, US discussion of these 'lessons' divided into two broad schools, the 'strategic' and the 'low-intensity', or, as one military author has classified them, the 'war' and the 'insurgency' schools. A third response to the apparent impasse of the 1970s was that of developing a strictly military strategy, based on a mix of 'smart' conventional weapons and low-yield nuclear missiles, for dealing with third world crises and threats. This thinking was evident behind the January 1988 Pentagon report on *Discriminate Deterrence*, in which a special emphasis on the threat of the third world to the USA was combined with discussion of how a selective, that is, 'discriminate', use of nuclear weapons could make military strategy in the third world viable again. In some ways the change in US perception of the third world threat in the 1980s made such neo-interventionist discussion easier. Once conflict in the third world was partially separated from the rivalry with the USSR, the overall strategic dangers of military action there were reduced. Selective strikes against 'terrorist' states, narcotics merchants in Latin America, or hijackers of civilian airliners, actions carried out on the pretext that these targets were the main enemy, made intervention 'thinkable' again in a way that would have been more difficult if such actions had involved large-scale commitments of US combat troops or the prospect of a direct clash with the Soviet Union.

Thus a report prepared by the Center for Strategic and International Studies at Georgetown designed to orientate policy for the next president was entitled: *Meeting the Mavericks: Regional Challenges to the Next President*. This document argued that while the threat of the USSR was receding, other threats in the third world were growing: from assertive regional powers, from the diffusion of new technologies, nuclear and conventional, and from a range of novel phenomena, which exposed 'unconventional vulnerability', such as terrorism, kidnapping and hijacking, and narcotics traffickers. In calling for 'unconventional responses' the report identified problems within the US system and political tradition, and in effect called for the removal of any remaining scruples: 'By contrast, the US response to unconventional attacks tends to be fashioned within its own democratic traditions, attempting to rely on the force of domestic and international law to deal with unconventional threats. Success at any price has never been a concept with which Americans are particularly comfortable. At the same time, defeat at every turn is not a prospect the United States should accept with equanimity. In the absence of any effective set of responses, the United States will remain vulnerable to the grey area of unconventional warfare'.[6] The characteristics of a new policy, containing many items on the new interventionist menu, included: making response to regional challenges a central, as distinct from reactive, component of US foreign policy; a policy of ensuring domestic support of such policies through 'public education'; expecting less from allies and clients; more systematic security assistance; developing ways of applying 'covert force' in the third world; using 'coercive diplomacy' more intelligently, avoiding the errors of some earlier involvements; a greater emphasis within the US national security organization on third world issues.

Behind the delicate formulations of the report, a more assertive agenda could be detected; 'public education' meant the kind of media manipulation and disinformation developed by the Reagan Administration with regard to Central America; reduced expectations of allies translated as less concern for diplomatic consequences and a more vigorous US unilateralism. What this report and so much of the new interventionism ignored was the political and international context in which these new problems emerged: for example, third world states were more assertive and aggressive because more developed countries, like the USA, sold them weapons; drug traffic boomed because of demand within the USA; terrorism was in many cases a response to long-festering political situations which the USA did little to ameliorate; third world upheavals had not a little to do with conditions of extreme social and political injustice maintained by régimes that had western backing, of precisely the 'security assistance' kind that the CSIS was proposing to augment.

In so much of the US discussion on third world intervention, however, there lay more nebulous but nonetheless potent factors of psychology and ideology. With the US on the rebound from the Vietnam defeat the prospect of intervention against others became acceptable again, provided the cost to the USA itself was not too high. The leitmotif of virtually all US public discussion of

Vietnam in the 1980s, be this in history books, films or political speeches, was the attempt to come to terms with what Vietnam did 'to us', – the USA; what it had done to Vietnam, when it left a devastated ecology, economy and human community compounded by a vindictive US blockade, was all too rarely touched on. This moral and historical solipsism was nowhere clearer than in the term most commonly used, by liberals as much as by interventionists, to describe the Vietnam involvement: 'quagmire'. This term, redolent of self-pity, implied that it was the USA which was the victim, and that had it not become 'stuck' in Vietnam, all would have been well. The question of whether the involvement itself had been legitimate, and of what it did to 'others', the inhabitants of the 'quagmire', was conveniently repressed.

Compromise and Beyond

Two conclusions, above all, follow from this analysis and from the shifting interaction of east-west and north-south relations discussed in this and previous chapters. The first is that since the causes of third world upheaval are to a considerable extent independent of Soviet–US rivalry they will continue irrespective of relations between Washington and Moscow. A detente of east and west that presupposes an end to third world crisis will be precarious, as will a policy which assumes that one panacea or another can cure the international effects of third world change. The contradiction into which the liberal non-interventionist position is driven illustrates all too clearly that social and political upheaval in the third world will endure and will inevitably spread in its effects: the maintenance of peace involves not preventing such upheaval but recognizing and living with its consequences on the international plane. As far as the Soviet–US relationship itself is concerned, the converse applies: that rivalry between the two, for all that it has acquired a third world component, is not only a product of regional challenges or misunderstandings but of a broader socio-economic competition that encompasses the arms race, the third world, and the pattern of social and political change within the blocs themselves. If it is this broader context that explains how and why the two power blocs became involved in the third world, it also indicates that a resolution of some merely 'regional' conflicts will not produce complete agreement. The appearance of diplomatic accord in the late 1980s resulted not from an end to Soviet–US rivalry, but rather from a shift in the balance of strength between the two sides, and from the need by the USSR to make concessions in the third world in order to concentrate its efforts on revitalization at home. It remained to be seen how far that revitalization would succeed, and how far the third world conflicts to which Soviet and US diplomacy were addressing themselves would permit solicitious co-operation between the great powers.

At the core of the Soviet–US rivalry there lay a competition between two political and social systems, two competing general ideas about how individual societies and the world as a whole should be organized. This competition, far from disappearing, was continuing through the late 1980s on precisely the terrain most central to it, around the forms of government and socio-economic system to be found in third world societies, and, by extension, in the more developed world. If by 'Cold War' is meant periods of intense Soviet–US rivalry, then the growth of negotiation on arms control and third world issues in the late 1980s meant an end to Cold War: but, used in this narrow way, the term is distinct from the broader dynamic of east-west rivalry that continues even when there is no 'Cold War' in the narrow sense. The Cold Wars of the late 1940s and early 1980s induced us to see the conflict as a predominantly military one, concerned with arms races, weapons supplies and local conflicts: important and in many respects autonomous as these were, they were always part of, and subordinate to, a broader socio-economic conflict that was equally manifested in economic performance, political campaigns, and ideological rivalry. There was little in the negotiations of the late 1980s to suggest that this underlying conflict had ended: much as they brought relief to specific regions and states, the negotiations, and the compromises they entailed, provided a new forum for the working out of the conflict and for the testing of the strength and resilience of each bloc and its third world allies.

APPENDIX 1

Basic principles of relations between the United States of America and the Union of Soviet Socialist Republics

Text of agreement, May 29 1972

The United States of America and the Union of Soviet Socialist Republics,

Guided by their obligations under the Charter of the United Nations and by a desire to strengthen peaceful relations with each other and to place these relations on the firmest possible basis,

Aware of the need to make every effort to remove the threat of war and to create conditions which promote the reduction of tensions in the world and the strengthening of universal security and international cooperation,

Believing that the improvement of US–Soviet relations and their mutually advantageous development in such areas as economics, science and culture, will meet these objectives and contribute to better mutual understanding and business-like cooperation, without in any way prejudicing the interests of third countries,

Conscious that these objectives reflect the interests of the peoples of both countries,

Have agreed as follows:

First. They will proceed from the common determination that in the nuclear age there is no alternative to conducting their mutual relations on the basis of peaceful coexistence.

Differences in ideology and in the social systems of the USA and the USSR are not obstacles to the bilateral development of normal relations based on the principles of sovereignty, equality, non-interference in internal affairs and mutual advantage.

Second. The USA and the USSR attach major importance to preventing the development of situations capable of causing a dangerous exacerbation of their relations. Therefore, they will do their utmost to avoid military confrontations and to prevent the outbreak of nuclear war. They will always exercise restraint in their mutual relations, and will be prepared to negotiate and settle differences by peaceful means. Discussions and negotiations on outstanding issues will be conducted in a spirit of reciprocity, mutual accommodation and mutual benefit.

Both sides recognize that efforts to obtain unilateral advantage at the expense of the other, directly or indirectly, are consistent with these objectives. The prerequisites for maintaining and strengthening peaceful relations between the USA and the USSR are the recognition of the security interests of the Parties based on the principle of equality and the renunciation of the use or threat of force.

Third. The USA and the USSR have a special responsibility, as do other countries which are permanent members of the United Nations Security Council, to do everything in their power so that conflicts or situations will not arise which would serve to increase international tensions. Accordingly, they will seek to promote conditions in which all countries will live in peace and security and will not be subject to outside interference in their internal affairs.

Fourth. The USA and the USSR intend to widen the juridical basis of their mutual relations and to exert the necessary efforts so that bilateral agreements which they have concluded and multilateral treaties and agreements to which they are jointly parties are faithfully implemented.

Fifth. The USA and the USSR reaffirm their readiness to continue the practice of exchanging views on problems of mutual interest and, when necessary, to conduct such exchanges at the highest level, including meetings between leaders of the two countries.

The two governments welcome and will facilitate an increase

in productive contacts between representatives of the legislative bodies of the two countries.

Sixth. The Parties will continue their efforts to limit armaments on a bilateral as well on a multilateral basis. They will continue to make special efforts to limit strategic armaments. Whenever possible, they will conclude concrete agreements aimed at achieving these purposes.

The USA and the USSR regard as the ultimate objective of their efforts the achievement of general and complete disarmament and the establishment of an effective system of international security in accordance with the purposes and principles of the United Nations.

Seventh. The USA and the USSR regard commercial and economic ties as an important and necessary element in the strengthening of their bilateral relations and thus will actively promote the growth of such ties. They will facilitate cooperation between the relevant organizations and enterprises of the two countries and the conclusion of appropriate agreements and contracts, including long-term ones.

The two countries will contribute to the improvement of maritime and air communications between them.

Eighth. The two sides consider it timely and useful to develop mutual contacts and cooperation in the fields of science and technology. Where suitable, the USA and the USSR will conclude appropriate agreements dealing with concrete cooperation in these fields.

Ninth. The two sides reaffirm their intention to deepen cultural ties with one another and to encourage fuller familiarization with each other's cultural values. They will promote improved conditions for cultural exchanges and tourism.

Tenth. The USA and the USSR will seek to ensure that their ties and cooperation in all the above-mentioned fields and in any others in their mutual interest are built on a firm and long-term basis. To give a permanent character to these efforts, they will establish in all fields where this is feasible joint commissions or other joint bodies.

Eleventh. The USA and the USSR make no claim for themselves and would not recognize the claims of anyone else to any special rights or advantages in world affairs. They recognize the sovereign equality of all states.

The development of US–Soviet relations is not directed against third countries and their interests.

Twelfth. The basic principles set forth in this document do not affect any obligations with respect to other countries earlier assumed by the USA and the USSR.

Moscow, *May 29, 1972*

For the United States
of America

Richard Nixon

President of the
United States
of America

For the Union of Soviet
Socialist Republics

Leonid I. Brezhnev

General Secretary of the
Central Committee,
CPSU

167

APPENDIX 2

Strategy for Low Intensity Conflict

From: *National Security Strategy of the United States*, The White House, January 1988

While high intensity conflict has been successfully deterred in most regions of primary strategic interest to the United States, low intensity conflicts continue to pose a variety of threats to the achievement of important US objectives. As described in last year's report, low intensity conflict typically manifests itself as political-military confrontation below the level of conventional war, frequently involving protracted struggles of competing principles and ideologies, and ranging from subversion to the direct use of military force. These conflicts, generally in the Third World, can have both regional and global implications for our national security interests. For example:

* Military basing, access and transit rights in the Philippines, key to US power projection capabilities in the Western Pacific and Indian Oceans, are presently threatened by the communist insurgency being waged against the Philippine Government.
* In mineral-rich southern Africa, insurgencies, economic instability and apartheid, as well as ethnic tribal conflicts, pose potential threats to the extraction of essential raw materials and their export to industries in the West and Japan. The conflicts endemic in the region are exacerbated by the activity of the Soviet Union and its surrogates.

* Soviet, Cuban and Nicaraguan support for insurgencies in El Salvador and elsewhere in Latin America threaten nascent democracies in the region which are already struggling with chronic poverty, economic underdevelopment, and the growing influence of narcotics cartels.
* Libya has used the threat of restricting or denying oil shipments to blunt West European response to state-sponsored terrorism, while simultaneously training terrorists on Libyan soil. Freedom of action for some US allies can be limited by economic ties.

Our strategies for dealing with low intensity conflict recognize that US responses in such situations must be realistic, if discreet, and founded on a clear relationship between the conflict's outcome and important US national security interests. Many low intensity conflicts have no direct relevance to those interests, while others may affect them in the most fundamental ways. When a US response is called for, we take care to ensure that it is developed in accordance with the principles of international and domestic law, which affirm the inherent right of states to use force in individual or collective self-defense against armed attack; and to assist one another in maintaining internal order against insurgency, terrorism, illicit narcotics traffic, and other characteristic forms of low intensity conflict.

Consistent with our strategies for dealing with low intensity conflict, *when it is in US interest to do so*, the United States will:

* Work to ameliorate the underlying causes of conflict in the Third World by promoting economic development and the growth of democratic political institutions.
* Support selected resistance movements opposing oppressive regimes working against US interests. Such support will be coordinated with friends and allies.
* Take measures to strengthen friendly nations facing internal or external threats to their independence and stability by employing appropriate instruments of US power. Where possible, action will be taken early – before instability leads to widespread violence; and emphasis will be placed on those measures which strengthen the threatened regime's long-term capability to deal with threats to its freedom and stability.

* Take steps to discourage Soviet and other state-sponsored adventurism, and increase the costs to those who use proxies or terrorist and subversive forces to exploit instability.
* Assist other countries in the interdiction and eradication of illicit narcotics production and traffic. Measures which have proven particularly effective include aid to expand and improve the affected country's law enforcement capabilities, to preserve the independence and integrity of its judicial system, and to provide for the sharing of intelligence and investigative capabilities.

Our own military forces have demonstrated capabilities to engage in low intensity conflict, and these capabilities have improved substantially in the last several years. But the most appropriate application of US military power is usually indirect through security assistance – training, advisory help, logistics support, and the supply of essential military support equipment. Recipients of such assistance bear the primary responsibility for promoting their own security interests with the US aid provided. Our program of assistance to El Salvador illustrates a successful indirect application of US military power.

The balanced application of the various elements of national power is necessary to protect US interests in low intensity conflicts. But in the final analysis, the tools we have at our disposal are of little use without the support of the American people, and their willingness to stay the course in what can be protracted struggles. We cannot prevail if there is a sharp asymmetry of wills – if our adversaries' determination is greater than our own. At the same time we do hold important advantages. We represent a model of political and economic development that promises freedom from political oppression and economic privation. If we can protect our own security, and maintain an environment of reasonable stability and open trade and communication throughout the Third World, political, economic, and social forces should eventually work to our advantage.

APPENDIX 3

Agreement between Afghanistan and Pakistan on the Principles of Mutual Relations, in Particular on Non-Interference and Non-Intervention

Geneva, April 1988

The Republic of Afghanistan and the Islamic Republic of Pakistan, hereinafter referred to as the High Contracting Parties.

Desiring to normalize relations and promote good-neighbourliness and co-operation as well as to strengthen international peace and security in the region.

Considering that full observance of the principles of non-interference and non-intervention in the internal and external affairs of States is of the greatest importance for the maintenance of international peace and security and for the fulfilment of the purposes and principles of the Charter of the United Nations.

Reaffirming the inalienable right of States freely to determine their own political, cultural and social systems in accordance with the will of their peoples, without outside intervention, interference, subversion, coercion or threat in any form whatsoever.

Mindful of the provisions of the Charter of the United Nations as well as the resolutions adopted by the United Nations on the principle of non-interference and non-intervention, in particular the Declaration on Principles of International Law concerning Friendly Relations and Co-operation among States in accordance with the Charter of the United Nations, of 24 October

1970, as well as the Declaration on the Inadmissability of Intervention in the Internal Affairs of States, of 9 December 1981
Have agreed as follows:

Article I

Relations between the High Contracting Parties shall be conducted in strict compliance with the principle of non-interference and non-intervention by States in the affairs of other States.

Article II

For the purpose of implementing the principle of non-interference and non-intervention each High Contracting Party undertakes to comply with the following obligations:

(1) to respect the sovereignty, political independence, territorial integrity, national unity, security and non-alignment of the other High Contracting Party, as well as the national identity and cultural heritage of its people;

(2) to respect the sovereign and inalienable right of the other High Contracting Party freely to determine its own political, economic, cultural and social systems, to develop its international relations and to exercise permanent sovereignty over its natural resources, in accordance with the will of its people, and without outside intervention, interference, subversion, coercion or threat in any form whatsoever;

(3) to refrain from the threat or use of force in any form whatsoever so as not to violate the boundaries of each other, to disrupt the political, social or economic order of the other High Contracting Party, to overthrow or change the political system of the other High Contracting Party or its Government, or to cause tension between the High Contracting Parties;

(4) to ensure that its territory is not used in any manner which would violate the sovereignty, political independence, territorial integrity and national unity or disrupt the political, economic and social stability of the other High Contracting Party;

(5) to refrain from armed intervention, subversion, military occupation or any other form of intervention and interference, overt or covert, directed at the other High Contracting Party, or any act of military, political or economic interference in

172

the internal affairs of the other High Contracting Party, including acts of reprisal involving the use of force;

(6) to refrain from any action or attempt in whatever form or under whatever pretext to destabilize or to undermine the stability of the other High Contracting Party or any of its institutions;

(7) to refrain from the promotion, encouragement or support, direct or indirect, of rebellious or secessionist activities against the other High Contracting Party, under any pretext whatsoever, or from any other action which seeks to disrupt the unity or to undermine or subvert the political order of the other High Contracting Party;

(8) to prevent within its territory the training, equipping, financing and recruitment of mercenaries from whatever origin for the purpose of hostile activities against the other High Contracting Party, or the sending of such mercenaries into the territory of the other High Contracting Party and accordingly to deny facilities, including financing for the training, equipping and transit of such mercenaries;

(9) to refrain from making any agreements or arrangements with other States designed to intervene or interfere in the internal and external affairs of the other High Contracting Party;

(10) to abstain from any defamatory campaign, vilification or hostile propaganda for the purpose of intervening or interfering in the internal affairs of the other High Contracting Party;

(11) to prevent any assistance to or use of or tolerance of terrorist groups, saboteurs or subversive agents against the other High Contracting Party;

(12) to prevent within its territory the presence, harbouring, in camps and bases or otherwise, organizing, training, financing, equipping and arming of individuals and political, ethnic and any other groups for the purpose of creating subversion, disorder or unrest in the territory of the other High Contracting Party and accordingly also to prevent the use of mass media and the transportation of arms, ammunition and equipment by such individuals and groups;

(13) not to resort to or to allow any other action that could be considered as interference or intervention.

Article III

The present Agreement shall enter into force on 15 May 1988.

Article IV

Any steps that may be required in order to enable the High Contracting Parties to comply with the provisions of Article II of this Agreement shall be completed by the date on which this Agreement enters into force.

Article V

This agreement is drawn up in English, Pashtu and Urdu languages, all texts being equally authentic. In case of any divergence of interpretation, the English text shall prevail.

Done in five original copies at Geneva this fourteenth day of April 1988.

(Signed by Afghanistan and Pakistan.)

APPENDIX 4

Fidel Castro: Rectification and Perestroika. Excerpts from speech on 35th Anniversary of Moncada, 26th July 1988

Source: Granma, Weekly edition, 7 August 1988

We read in the papers that other socialist countries are analyzing their history, their performance, their work; they're trying to overcome their difficulties. There's never been a period in history in which a social regime, a social system has in such a short time achieved such huge accomplishments as socialism has; yet there'll always be, when it comes to any human endeavor, material for criticism, for analysis and for overcoming the difficulties. A revolutionary never feels satisfied, nor can he ever feel that way; he must be eternally dissatisfied.

It was following the 3rd Congress of our Party, which very realistically, clearly and courageously analyzed our difficulties, our mistakes and our negative tendencies, that this process of rectification began. More or less simultaneously, the same thing happened in the Soviet Union and in other socialist countries, without anyone having agreed to do so beforehand.

There are some people who believe that what's being done in other places is what we ought to start doing right away, and there are also some brains around – people who have no confidence in themselves, no confidence in their nation, no confidence in their people, no confidence in their Revolution – who right away say we have to copy what others are doing. (APPLAUSE) That's an incorrect stand, a wrong stand because no two revolutionary processes are the same, no two countries are the same no two histories are the same, no two idiosyncracies are the same. Some have certain problems, others have other problems; some make certain mistakes, others make other mistakes.

If someone has a toothache, why would he use a cure for corns? Or if his corns hurt, why must he use a cure for a toothache? That's why our measures are not the same, nor can they be the same as those used by other countries and it would be entirely wrong for us to look for the same solutions or mechanically copy the other countries' solutions.

One thing I ought to say here: that this revolution was precisely characterized by a reluctance to copy from others but instead by creativeness. (APPLAUSE) Had we been willing to follow stereotypes, we wouldn't be gathered here today, we wouldn't have had a 26th of July, we wouldn't have had a socialist revolution in this hemisphere, perhaps there wouldn't have been any yet. Had we been willing to follow stereotypes, theory had it that no revolution could have been made here; that's what theory used to say, that's what the books used to say, what the manuals used to say. Let it be well understood: that's what theory, books, manuals used to say!

Our situation wasn't worse than that of other Latin American countries: Cuba's objective economic and social conditions, however bad they were – and they were indeed bad – didn't resemble the objective conditions of other Latin America countries much worse off. And today we see that no socialist revolution has yet been made in those countries.

I make one exception here – and I'm not placing it in the category of a socialist revolution but in whatever category they may wish to place it in, but I consider it a true and profound revolution – I make the exception of the Nicaraguan Revolution. (APPLAUSE) It is only up to them to know how things should be done there, how problems should be tackled.

Recently, Daniel (Ortega) spoke about the essence, the character or the socialist sense of the Nicaraguan Revolution and that caused a lot of noise, and he was only speaking about the essence, the character, the sense of the process, he didn't say it was a socialist revolution.

So, then, there's been none other in the rest of Latin America, where all the problems that I was mentioning here remain. There are some places where every year 100 children die per 1000 live births, and in some other places the number is 150 and even 200. Infant mortality in very few countries there is below 60. Prostitution, drugs, begging, poverty are everywhere. Rickets, mal-nutrition, children without schools, young people unemployed and without universities are everywhere and there's been no revolution.

The thing is that a revolution depends on many circumstances and making one is not easy in any sense.

Had we said: let's wait for a huge economic crisis to break out in Cuba, like the one under dictator Machado or even worse than that one, and let starvation drive people to rise up, we would still be waiting. Yet we did draw our own conclusions starting out from the principles of socialism, of Marxism–Leninism – not from pamphlets – and we said: there are objective conditions in Cuba for a revolution, what's missing are subjective conditions. Our people have special characteristics. The subjective conditions for the revolution could be created because there were objective conditions present.

It wasn't a whim for we were thinking about the Revolution even before March 10, 1952 (the date of Batista's coup). We would have have tried to follow the revolution even before March 10 (APPLAUSE) and in a revolution with the people, in a profound revolution, in a revolution that sooner or later had to become a socialist revolution – for we couldn't conceive a different type of revolution in our country, dominated by neocolonialism, dominated by imperialism, in this country where nearly all the sugar mills, railroads, mines, ports, best lands, electricity, telephones, rubber, everything, belonged to foreigners. We were but a colony, worse than a colony!

Starting out from, I'd say, two currents of thought, starting out – to be more exact – from Marxist-Leninist thought and Marti's thought, starting out from a true appraisal of our people, their characteristics, their history, the objective realities that afflicted them, even if they weren't as bad as those that afflicted other countries on our continent, we arrived at the conclusion that the revolution was possible in our country, which is why our country, that was the last one – the last one! – to free itself from

Spain, became the first one to free itself from US imperialism in this hemisphere, the first one! And the first one to carry out a socialist revolution. (APPLAUSE)

I'd like to know what some of those second-rate copiers and imitators would have done under circumstances similar to those that existed here before July 26. We could place them in similar circumstances, from which our Revolution started out and see what they'd do.

That's why I say that the first major test that showed that ours was a creative revolution is that it didn't follow stereotypes and that in constructing socialism our Revolution made many contributions while remaining faithful to the principles of Marxism–Leninism: the principle of combining study and work, for instance, proclaimed by Marx stemming from the history of the British working class whose exploited children were turned into a productive force, conceived the idea that under socialism study and work could and ought to be combined, and Marti, on the basis of his familiarity with our people's characteristics and reality, said the same thing. Our country was the first one in the world in massively and reasonably applying those principles and today we see the fruits in the behaviour of our youth, because it isn't by chance that our new generation display the revolutionary attributes we see in them.

This principle has been applied for the past 25 years. We have already whole generations – every young person 35 years old or under, has in one way or another taken part in programs combining study and work. That's why when called upon to join a particular project, or do voluntary work, they are not afraid. That was proof of our Revolution's creative spirit.

The powerful mass organizations created by our Revolution also attested to that creative spirit; the Committees for the Defense of the Revolution, the Federation of Cuban Women – not as a committee at the top but a grass-roots organization – were created by the Revolution; and the peasant organization. I'm not talking about something that already existed like the workers organized in trade unions. No other revolution relied on the mass organizations of our Revolution and which other revolutions that came later tried to use as an experience. The Committees for the Defense of the Revolution now exist in several Third World countries that have made their own revolution.

The manner in which an agrarian reform was carried out in our country differed from the manner in which all the other socialist countries carried it out because they all divided up the land and we didn't. Had we divided up the big cattle ranches or the sugar plantations in small lots or tiny parcels, today we wouldn't be supplying calories for 40 million people. We kept those land units intact and developed them as big production enterprises. We gave land to the peasant who was in possession of it to sharecroppers, tenant farmers and others. We said to them all here you are, the land is yours and subsequently we haven't forced any of them to join cooperatives. The process of uniting those plots has taken us 30 years, we've gone ahead little by little on the basis of the strict principle of it being voluntary. There can't be a single peasant in Cuba who can say that he was forced to join a cooperative, there can't be any! And yet, over two-thirds of their land now belong to cooperatives, and all of them are making headway, they are prospering. On the other hand, 80 per cent of the land in our country belongs to state farms whose self-sufficiency is collective. The cooperatives are also self-sufficient. It was a different road they took.

Our Revolution – and this no one can deny – has been kept going with tremendous ideological strength because who can defend us? Were imperialism to attack us, who is therefore to defend the island? No one will come from abroad to defend the island: we defend the island ourselves. (APPLAUSE) It isn't that someone might not want to defend us, the thing is that no one can because this socialist revolution is not just a few kilometers away from the Soviet Union; this socialist revolution is 10,000 kilometers away from the Soviet Union.

Were the revolutionary process in Cuba to suffer a crisis, who would save it? Will imperialism come to save the revolutionary process? Were the revolutionary process in Cuba to be weakened, who would save it?

That's why all that we do has exceptional importance. It isn't that we want to be more virtuous than anybody else or purer than anybody else, but that we are 90 miles away from the most powerful empire on earth and 10,000 miles from the socialist camp. We are two millimeters away from the empire, right there at the Guantanamo naval base and that's why the empire is trying to weaken the Revolution ideologically, that's

179

why it is campaigning so much, making so much propaganda, to try to sow distrust, doubt, division, weaken the Revolution and swallow it like a ripe apple. They said that in centuries past and devised the theory of the ripe apple. But they haven't succeeded despite all their planning and plotting nor will they succeed in undermining it from within.

That's why I can only feel contempt for those who allow themselves to be carried away by silly things and illusions, those with a weak heart, a weak brain, a weak will who are unable to grasp these realities.

I believe that our country has carried out an extraordinary historical feat on building socialism in the geographical conditions in which it has done so and that's why we must watch over the ideological purity of the Revolution, the ideological solidity of the Revolution. (APPLAUSE) That's why we can't use mechanisms, any kind of tools smacking of capitalism: this is an essential question of the Revolution's survival, that is why the Revolution must resolutely stick to the purest principles of Marxism–Leninism and Marti's thought, stick to them rather than playing around or flirting with the things of capitalism.

We believe in socialism and do so profoundly! (APPLAUSE) Because socialism has changed our nation, we are able to do a lot more because the fact that we can speak today about these and other things, housing, shantytowns that can be demolished in no time, water, food, education and health for all, industrial and agricultural development, is because we are the owners of our country, because socialism made us the owners of our country, socialism made us the owners of our lands, our sugar mills, our factories, our mines, of everything, and that's why we can say: let's get to work, let's do this or the other, anything. Could we do this in a capitalist society or in a caricature of capitalism like this country used to be, in a Yankee neocolony?

We believe in socialism and, therefore, we must be very careful when interpreting and applying the theory: we must be very careful in every step we take. And the Revolution was always like that, it is now almost 30 and it looks healthy, full of pep, strong, 90 miles from the United States. (APPLAUSE)

That's why every country on the basis of its own history, its concrete experiences, must draw up its own formulas, and we respect the formulas drawn up by each country, we have the fullest respect for them. We are glad of the efforts being made by the socialist countries to overcome their difficulties, the problems that have been created for them throughout history; yet there are many problems that arose in the other countries which didn't arise in our country; our problems are different, of another type, precisely because we do not copy from others, because we were creative and didn't simply copy from others.

I've on occasion even criticized our having had so much zeal for applying our own interpretations that we neglected using the positive experiences of the socialist countries; but we also occasionally copied negative experiences of the socialist countries and that's the truth. Now we'll go on searching for our own path, our own formulas; we'll always go on paying attention to what any socialist country does that can be useful to us, and we'll go on being reluctant to abjectly copy prescriptions to remedy ills we've never been afflicted with. And, needless to say, we do not only wish but need the socialist countries to succeed in their efforts to overcome their difficulties, and I trust they'll be successful, for I've never been pessimistic, I have great confidence in socialism and I believe we all do because we have proof and reasons for that confidence.

I believe that socialism has accomplished extraordinary things – what the Soviet Union did has no precedent, what the Soviet people did has no precedent, starting with the Great October Revolution; their resistance against generalized invasion by all the capitalist countries following World War I; their industrialization; their resistance against fascism; the 20 million lives they lost in saving socialism and saving humanity from fascism; a country that had hardly been constructed when it was destroyed and they rebuilt it again; a country that achieved nuclear parity with imperialism, an incredible feat; a country whose space-ships are right now headed for the satellites of Mars. We're familiar with their successes. That more can be achieved? Yes, that's true. That we must try to do better? Of course. But we do not deny nor will we ever permit others to deny the colossal successes achieved by socialism. I say this because the imperialists, on the basis of the self-criticism now going on in the socialist countries and the Soviet Union, are bent on discrediting everything that socialism has accomplished; they're trying to discredit everything that socialism has done, to detract from the historical merits of socialism and demoralize it.

If I were asked, I know the flaws that, in my opinion, it has, and some of them I have thought over many times, but it is not up to me to proclaim the problems of others because everyone has to analyze and solve their own problems. I could even say what equipment has difficulties, but I can also speak about many good and marvelous things about socialist technology and socialist equipment.

... The imperialists are trying to reap a good harvest with this process of criticism and self-criticism now going on in the socialist countries and they are bent on sowing demoralization. Many capitalists believe that the socialists will have no choice but to adopt methods, styles and even motivations and a certain kind of idiosyncracy of a capitalist nature. They're indulging in troubled waters. They're even trying to blame us for the fact that we're not doing things exactly the same way that the Soviets are doing them, in order to create intrigue, to try to divide us.

Of course, it would be in their interest to pit us one against the other or drive a wedge between Cubans and Soviets. However, never before has our communication been greater, our communication with the leadership of the Soviet Party is excellent, we understand each other perfectly, we speak a frank and clear language, and it has never occurred to us to think that we simply have to copy what the Soviets do; nor has it occurred to the Soviet leadership to think that we have to copy what they're doing. That's clear.

Returning to the essential idea here: everyone must have the right to do what is convenient for them.

I am hoping that in this process the socialist countries, if they make mistakes, are capable of correcting those mistakes; because they will unquestionably make mistakes in the process, yet I'm confident that they will try to rectify them. And that's what we said concerning what we're doing: we must be able to rectify not just the mistakes made and the negative tendencies but also rectify the mistakes we may make in the process of rectification itself!

What I can indeed tell the imperialists and the theoreticians of imperialism is that Cuba will never adopt methods, styles, philosophies or characteristics of capitalism. That I can indeed tell them! (APPLAUSE) Capitalism has had some technological successes, some successes in organization, there are some things in their technology or some organizational experiences that are diametrically different, by definition and by essence.

We're proud of the ideological purity, of the ideological strength of a country that has confronted imperialism; and not just confronted imperialism but a country where hundreds and thousands of its people have fulfilled internationalist missions, a country where one only has to raise his hand and if 10,000 teachers are needed for Nicaragua, all 10,000 teachers turn up to go to Nicaragua; (APPLAUSE) if doctors are needed, doctors go there; a country that when fighters were needed has always had ten times more fighters willing to fulfill the mission than the number of fighters actually needed.

That's why today, on this 35th anniversary, one very basic idea is never to forget where we are located, we're not in the Black Sea but in the Caribbean Sea, not 90 miles from Odessa but 90 miles from Miami, with our land bordering on imperialism in an occupied portion of our territory. Our people are responsible for our country and our Party is responsible for its policy, its line, its defense.

NOTES

Introduction

1. The rise to dominance of Japanese capitalism within the contemporary world has ominous implications far beyond its strictly economic impact, which is a normal part of inter-state and inter-capitalist competition. In the case of US hegemony, the many negative features of that dominance were, in part at least, offset by the positive political and cultural features of the US system, as was evident in the impact of US radical current on western Europe: most of the alternative forms of political action developed in Europe in the 1960s and onwards originated in the USA – student militancy, black power, civil rights, the women's movement, ecology, demands for freedom of information. To this was added the many-sided stimulus of much of American culture, in its musical, literary and aesthetic forms. The Japanese state, by contrast, had projected a capitalist conformism with few such compensatory dimensions: of an almost monolithically racist, sexist and imperialist régime, within which the powerful alternative Japanese voices on issues such as nuclear weapons and ecology are denied international expression. Even Japan's supposedly most acceptable traditional export, flower arrangement, is a social construction designed to reinforce the subjugation and domestication of women. On the continuities between Japanese pre- and post-war international roles see Jon Halliday and Gavan MacCormack, *Japanese Imperialism Today*, Penguin 1973.
2. I am grateful to my colleagues in the Transnational Institute, especially Pedro Vilanova, Mariano Aguirre and Susan George for drawing the French and Spanish dimensions of this 'anti-third worldism' to my attention.
3. *The Making of the Second Cold War*, Verso 1983, second edition 1986.
4. On the GI practice of collecting chopped-off bits of their Vietnamese victims, see Michael Herr, *Dispatches*, Picador 1979.

Chapter 1

1. On the wars of the post-1945 period see Andrew Wilson, *The Disarmer's Handbook*, London 1983, pp. 31–35 and Evan Luard, *The Blunted Sword*, London 1988, pp. 61–68. See also Istvan Kende, 'Wars of Ten Years (1967–1976)', *Journal of Peace Research*, no. 3, vol. XV, 1978.
2. On the link between the arms race and third world conflict see Jonathan Steele, 'East–West and North–South' in Dan Smith and E.P. Thompson, eds., *Prospectus for a Habitable Planet*, London 1987.

3. On the 1972 Basic Principles agreement see Appendix 1, p. 171, and Raymond Garthoff, *Detente and Confrontation*, Washington 1985, pp. 290–298.
4. The fourteen revolutions were: Vietnam, Laos, Cambodia, Afghanistan, Iran, Ethiopia, Angola, Mozambique, Guinea-Bissau, Sao Tome, Cape Verde, Zimbabwe, Grenada, Nicaragua. See Chapter 2 for further discussion.
5. For proposals on how US arms policy and disarmament positions should be linked to broader US strategy towards the USSR see Zbigniew Brezezinski, *Game Plan*, New York 1986.
6. Susan Strange, *Casino Capitalism*, Oxford 1987.
7. On the weaknesses of the NAM, see my 'The Maturing of the Non-Aligned: perspectives from New Delhi', *Third World Affairs*, 1985.
8. For a general argument in favour of bipolarity see Kenneth Waltz, *Theory of International Politics*, New York 1979, pp. 170–176.

Chapter 2

1. On the international causes of revolutions, and in particular the international weakening of states through competition with others, see Theda Skocpol, *States and Social Revolutions*, Princeton 1979.
2. I have discussed this wave of revolutions more fully in my *The Making of the Second Cold War*, London 1983, Chapter 4.
3. Chalmers Johnson, *Autopsy on People's War*, California University Press, 1973.
4. For the analysis of the political dimensions of guerrilla war see Raymond Aron, *Clausewitz*, London 1983, Chapters 11–12; Andrew Mack, 'Why Big Nations Lose Small Wars: The Politics of Asymmetric Conflict', *World Politics*, May 1975; Goran Therborn, 'From Petrograd to Saigon', *New Left Review* 48, 1967, and Gabriel Kolko's analysis of Vietnam, *Anatomy of a War*, New York 1985
5. For a graphic account of the Cuban expedition to Angola see Gabriel Garcia Marquez, 'Operation Carlota', *New Left Review*, nos. 101/102, February–April 1977.
6. The US role in the 1964 Brazilian coup has been well documented. In Chile, the CIA was directly involved in trying to prevent Allende from taking power in 1970 and in aiding the opposition between then and 1973: no direct involvement in the 1973 coup has, to date, been demonstrated. The Pakistani military leaders who took power in 1977 were in close contact with the US embassy: the long record of military takeovers in that country indicates, however, that the anti-democratic forces had deep internal roots.
7. For a discussion of this process see Jorge Nef, 'The Trend toward Democratization and Redemocratization in Latin America: Shadow and Substance', *Latin American Research Review*, vol. XXIII, no. 3, 1988;

Edward Herman and James Petras, 'Resurgent Democracy: Rhetoric and Reality' *New Left Review*, no. 154, November–December 1985; and Paul Cammack's critique of Herman and Petras in *New Left Review*, no. 157, May–June 1980.

8. On this question see Bruce Cumings, *The Origins of the Korean War*, Princeton 1981, vol. 1, and Jon Halliday and Bruce Cumings, *Korea, The Unknown War*, New York 1988, Chapter 1.

9. On theories of revolutionary socialist transformation and self-reliance see: Gordon White, Robin Murray and Christine White, *Revolutionary Socialist Development in the Third World*, Brighton 1983; *World Development*, special issue on 'Socialism and Development', vol. 9, nos. 9/10, 1981.

10. *The Guardian*, 12 June 1988.

11. See *Le Monde*, 3 January 1989.

12. On the background to the Grenadian revolution and its place in the context of third world revolt see my 'Cold War in the Caribbean', *New Left Review*, no. 141, September–October 1983. A measured assessment of the strengths and weaknesses of Bishop as a leader is given by Richard Hart, attorney-general in the NJM government, in the introduction to *Maurice Bishop Speaks*, London 1985. The sectarian support for Bernard Coard and other opponents of Bishop which emerged from much of the Caribbean left after the October 1983 crisis in Grenada, justified by a misplaced 'anti-imperialism', compounded the setback to the idea of socialism which the Grenadian events represented throughout the region.

13. On the background to ideas of 'self-reliance', see Dieter Senghaas, *The European Experience*, Essex 1985.

14. For an inside account of the PDPA see Raja Anwar, *The Tragedy of Afghanistan*, London 1988.

15. Richard Fagen, Carmen Diana Deere, and Jose Luis Coraggio, eds., *Transition and Development, Problems of Third World Socialism*, New York 1986, especially the Chapter by E.V.K. Fitzgerald.

16. See the chapter by Barbara Stallings in Fagen *et al*, ed.

17. Skocpol, *States*, is especially clear on the degree to which revolutions *strengthen* states, a point too many analysts and supporters of revolution ignore.

18. On 'asymmetric conflict' see Andrew Mack, note 4 above.

Chapter 3

1. For a guide to this literature see Major Michael Brown, 'Vietnam, Learning from the Debate', *Military Review*, February 1987.

2. On the Reagan Doctrine, Uri Ra'anan and others, *Third World Marxist-Leninist Regimes: Strengths, Vulnerabilities and US Policy*, Institute for Foreign Policy Analysis, Washington 1985; Charles Krauthammer, 'The Reagan Doctrine', *Time* 1 April 1985; also 'The Reagan Doctrine', Insight section, *The Washington Times*, 10 March 1986, and Jeane Kirkpatrick, '*The*

Reagan Doctrine and U.S. Policy, The Heritage Foundation, 1985. Critical assessments of the Doctrine include: Michael Klare, Peter Kornbluh, eds., *Low-Intensity Warfare*, New York 1987; Tom Barry, *Low Intensity Conflict: The New Battlefield in Central America*, Inter-Hemispheric Educational Resource Centre, 1986; Ted Galen Carpenter, *US Aid to Anti-Communist Rebels: The 'Reagan Doctrine' and its Pitfalls*, Cato Institute, 1986; NACLA, Report on the Americas, *The Real War: Low Intensity Conflict in Central America* vol. XX, no. 2, April/May 1986; Michael Klare, 'The New U.S. Strategic Doctrine', *The Nation*, 28 December, 1985.

3. Michael Armacost, Under Secretary for Political Affairs, State Department, 8 April 1986, 'Dealing with Gorbachev's Soviet Union', US Department of State, Bureau of Public Affairs, *Current Policy* No. 825.

4. John Sewell, Richard Feinberg, Valeriana Kallab, eds., *US Foreign Policy and the Third World: Agenda 1985–6*, Overseas Development Council, New Brunswick 1986.

5. See R. Keohane and J. Nye, 'Two cheers for Multi-lateralism', *Foreign Policy*, No. 60, Fall 1985.

6. 'Low-Intensity Warfare: The Challenge of Ambiguity', U.S. Department of State, Bureau of Public Affairs, *Current Policy*, No. 783.

7. Donald Morelli and Michael Ferguson, 'Low-Intensity Conflict: An Operational Perspective', *Military Review*, November 1984, page 7. For an earlier British conceptualisation see Frank Kitson, *Low Intensity Operations, Subversion, Insurgency and Peacekeeping*, 1971.

8. For a cogent analysis of LIC in these terms see the NACLA report mentioned in note 1. I am especially grateful to Dan Siegel for clarifying this point to me.

9. Gregory Treverton, *Covert Action*, London 1987 for an overview.

10. Michael Klare, Peter Kornbluh, eds., *Low-Intensity Warfare*.

11. *IHT*, 10 March 1986.

12. *IHT*, 11 January 1985.

13. Shirley Christian, *Nicaragua, Revolution in the Family*, 1985.

14. An overview of the issues and confusions involved in the discussion of 'terrorism' is given by Eqbal Ahmad, 'Comprehending Terror', *MERIP Middle East Reports*, May–June 1986.

15. Michael Klare, *The Nation*, 25 February 1984.

16. The base system on land has been supplemented by an extensive system of Maritime Prepositioning Ships: thirteen of those in the Indian Ocean carry 30 days worth of fuel, ammunition and spare parts for the Marine Corps division.

Chapter 4

1. *Soviet News* 17 November 1982, for a list of those attending Brezhnev's funeral.

2. Brezhnev at the 26th CPSU Congress, *Soviet News* 24 February 1981.

3. For detailed discussion of Soviet policy on the third world, and in particular on debates amongst Soviet experts prior to 1985, see Jerry Hough, *The Struggle for the Third World*, Brookings Institution 1986; Galia Golan, *The Soviet Union and National Liberation Movements in the Third World*, London 1988; Elizabeth Valkenier, 'Revolutionary Change in the Third World: Recent Soviet Reassessments', *World Politics*, Vol. XXXVIII. April 1986, and her 'New Soviet Thinking about the Third World', *World Policy Journal*, Fall 1987.

4. On the theory of 'correlation of forces' see Margot Light, *The Soviet Theory of International Relations*, Chapter 8, Brighton 1988.

5. Thus in the November 1983 UN vote on Afghanistan only twelve third world states voted with the USSR: Afghanistan, Angola, Cuba, South Yemen, Ethiopia, Laos, Libya, Madagascar, Mongolia, Mozambique, Syria, Vietnam. Fourteen others abstained: Algeria, Benin, Burkina, Cape Verde, Congo-Brazzaville, Guinea-Bissau, India, Iraq, Malawi, Mali, Nicaragua, Sao Tome, Seychelles, Uganda.

6. Aleksei Kiva, 'Socialist Orientation: Reality and Illusions', *International Affairs*, July 1988, p. 83.

7. See my *Revolution and Foreign Policy: the Case of South Yemen*, Cambridge 1989, Chapter 5.

8. On this see Hough Chapter 8, Valkenier 1987, and Golan, Chapter 3 and pp. 236–43.

9. Mikhail Gorbachev, *Perestroika*, Collins 1988, pp. 146–7.

10. *Perestroika* p. 137.

11. Kiva, op. cit., provides a scathing critique of socialist-oriented states and of those who promoted them within the USSR. 'The salient feature of the bureaucratic approach in the years of stagnation was wishful thinking', he argues (p. 84). For further disparagement of third world states, see 'The USSR and the Third World', *International Affairs*, no. 12, 1988.

12. *New Times*, Vol. 23, June 1988, p. 16–17.

13. *Financial Times*, 4 August 1988.

14. Yevgeni Primakov, 'USSR Policy on Regional Conflicts', *International Affairs*, no. 6, 1988.

15. *Programme of the Communist Party of the Soviet Union*, New Edition, 1 March 1986, Novosti 1986, p. 71.

16. Kiva, op. cit. p. 84. Valkenier, 1987 op. cit., shows how the Soviet view of third world capitalism began to change as early as 1975.

17. *Perestroika* pp. 188–9. In the 1986 Programme discussion of Soviet relations with the third world, the term 'internationalism' is restricted to Soviet relations with those fighting racism and apartheid (p. 72).

18. Mengistu Haile-Mariam, *Responding to International Media*, 28 May 1988, Ministry of Information, Press Department, Addis Ababa, July 1988, pp. 40–1.

Chapter 5

1. I have gone into this in greater detail in my *The Making of the Second Cold War*, Verso second edition 1986.
2. *International Herald Tribune*, 29 July 1988.

Chapter 6

1. An illustrative example of this new bipartisan approach is given in Henry Kissinger and Cyrus Vance, 'Bipartisan Objectives for American Foreign Policy', *Foreign Affairs* summer 1988, where a calibrated interventionism is advocated.
2. For Shevardnadze on the need to pursue 'national interest' see 'Foreign Policy and Diplomacy', *International Affairs*, no. 10, 1988. For an outspoken example of 'international *glasnost*' and its denial of inherent conflict with the USA see Andrei Kozyrev, 'Confidence and the Balance of Interests', *International Affairs* no. 11, 1988.
3. For a comparison of Soviet and western ideas on 'interdependence' and related matters see the joint publication of IMEMO and the Royal Institute of International Affairs, *International Economic Security*, by Igor Artemiev and Fred Halliday, Moscow and London, 1988.
4. American Committee on US–Soviet Relations, *The Requirements for Stable Coexistence in US–Soviet Relations*, joint report with the USA–Canada Institute of the Academy of Sciences of the USSR, Washington 1988, p. 9.
5. On South Yemen and other cases of supposed Soviet 'expansionism' in the late 1970s see my *Threat from the East?*, Penguin 1982, published in the USA as *Soviet Policy in the Arc of Crisis*, Institute for Policy Studies 1981.
6. *Meeting the Mavericks*, p. 29.

BIBLIOGRAPHY

Anwar, Raja, *The Tragedy of Afghanistan, a First-Hand Account*, Verso, 1988

Barry, Tom, *Low Intensity Conflict, The New Battlefield in Central America*, Inter-Hemispheric Education Resource Center, 1986

Brittain, Victoria, *Hidden Lives, Hidden Deaths, South Africa's Crippling of a Continent*, Faber and Faber, 1988

Brzezinski, Zbigniew, *Game Plan, a Geostrategic Framework for the Conduct of the US–Soviet Contest*, Atlantic Monthly Press, 1986

Bull, Hedley, ed., *Intervention in World Politics*, Oxford, 1984

Cassen, Robert, ed., *Soviet Interests in the Third World*, Sage/RIIA, 1985

Chomsky, Noam, *Turning the Tide, US Intervention in Central America and the Struggle for Peace*, Pluto, 1985

Fagen, Richard, *Forging Peace, the Crisis of Central America*, Blackwells, 1987

Fagen, Richard, Deere, Carmen Diana and Coraggio, Jose Luis, eds., *Transition and Development, Problems of Third World Socialism*, Monthly Review Press, 1986

Ferguson, Thomas, and Rogers, Joel, *Right Turn, The Decline of the Democrats and the Future of American Politics*, Hill and Wang, 1986

Garthoff, Raymond, *Detente and Confrontation, American-Soviet Relations from Nixon to Reagan*, Brookings Institution, 1985

Garthoff, Raymond, *Reflections on the Cuban Missile Crisis*, Brookings Institution, 1987

Golan, Galia, *The Soviet Union and National Liberation Movements in the Third World*, Unwin Hyman, 1988

Gorbachev, Mikhail, *Perestroika, New Thinking for Our Country and the World*, Collins, 1987

Gresh, Alain, 'L'Union Sovietique face aux conflits regionaux: une diplomatie a l'epreuve du tiers monde', *Le Monde Diplomatique*, December 1988

Haig, Alexander, *Caveat: Realism, Reagan and Foreign Policy*, Weidenfeld and Nicholson, 1984

Halliday, Fred, *The Making of the Second Cold War*, second edition, Verso, 1986

BIBLIOGRAPHY

Halliday, Fred, *Threat from the East? Soviet Policy from Afghanistan and Iran to the Horn of Africa*, Penguin, 1982; published in the USA as *Soviet Policy in the Arc of Crisis*, Institute for Policy Studies, 1981

Harris, Nigel, *The End of the Third World*, Penguin, 1986

Hippler, Jochen, *Krieg im Frieden, Amerikanische Strategien fur die Dritte Welt*, Pahl-Rugenstein, 1986

Hippler, Jochen, 'Low-Intensity Warfare: Key Strategy for the Third World Theater', *MERIP Middle East Report*, vol. 17, no. 1, January–February, 1987

Hough, Jerry, *The Struggle for the Third World, Soviet Debates and American Options*, Brookings Institution, 1986

Ikle, Fred and Wohlstetter, Albert, *Discriminate Deterrence, Report of the Commission on Integrated Long-Term Strategy*, Department of Defense, 1988

Klare, Michael, *Beyond the 'Vietnam Syndrome'*, Institute for Policy Studies, 1982

Klare, Michael, *Supplying Repression*, Institute for Policy Studies, 1982

Klare, Michael and Kornbluh, Peter, *Low Intensity Warfare, Counterinsurgency, Proinsurgency and Antiterrorism in the Eighties*, Pantheon Books, 1988

Kolko, Gabriel, *Anatomy of a War, Vietnam, the US and the Modern Historical Experience*, Pantheon, 1985

Landau, Saul, *The Dangerous Doctrine, National Security and US Foreign Policy*, Westview Press, 1988

Ledeen, Michael, *Grave New World*, Oxford, 1985

Light, Margot, *The Soviet Theory of International Relations*, Harvester, 1986

Litwak, Robert, *Detente and the Nixon Doctrine, American Foreign Policy and the Pursuit of Stability, 1969–1976*, Cambridge University Press, 1984

MacFarlane, Neil, *Superpower Rivalry and Third World Radicalism: the Idea of National Liberation*, Croom Helm, 1985

Marcou, Lily, *Les Défis de Gorbachev*, Plon, 1988

Morley, Morris, ed., *Crisis and Confrontation, Ronald Reagan's Foreign Policy*, Rowman and Littlefield, 1988

Ra'anan, Uri *et al*, *Third World Marxist-Leninist Regimes: Strengths, Vulnerabilities and US Policy*, Institute for Foreign Policy Analysis, 1985

Sewell, John, Feinberg, Richard, and Kallab, Valeriana, *US Foreign Policy and the Third World; Agenda 1985–86*, Transaction Books/Overseas Development Council, 1985

Shearman, Peter, and Williams, Phil, eds., *The Superpowers, Central America and the Middle East*, Brassey's, 1988

Shulman, Marshall, ed., *East–West Tensions in the Third World*, W.W. Norton, 1986

Treverton, Gregory, *Covert Action, The CIA and American Intervention in the Postwar World*, I.B. Tauris, 1987

Valkenier, Elizabeth, 'Revolutionary Change in the Third World: Recent Soviet Reassessments', *World Politics*, vol. XXXVIII, April 1986

van Opstal, Debra, and Goldberg, Andrew, *Meeting the Mavericks: Regional Challenges for the Next President*, Center for Strategic and International Studies, Significant Issues Series, vol. X, no. 7, 1988

Woodward, Bob, *Veil: the Secret Wars of the CIA*, Simon and Schuster 1988.

INDEX

Addis Ababa 131, 138

Afghanistan 9, 15, 24, 25, 29, 34, 43, 45, 47, 48, 50, 53, 54, 59, 76, 77, 79, 80, 87, 92, 93, 95, 101, 103, 107, 108, 109, 110, 118, 119, 121, 123, 128, 130, 131, 133, 134, 135, 136, 139, 141, 142, 143, 144, 150, 152, 158, 159; *Mujahidin* 78, 87, 88, 93; People's Democratic Party of (PDPA) 43, 47, 107, 121, 130, 147, 148

Africa 11, 26, 29, 36, 100, 126; *see also* countries

African National Congress (ANC) 86, 128

Algeria 24, 27, 29, 120, 126, 143, 144, 145; POLISARIO 144

Al-Huss, Salim 146

Alliance for Progress (in S. America) 64

Al-Mahdi, Sadiq 82

Al-Nimeiry, President (Sudan) 82

Amin, Idi 122

Andoprov, Yuri 15, 17, 101, 111, 112

Angola 9, 24, 25, 27, 29, 31, 34, 36, 37, 39, 46, 49, 54, 57, 59, 75, 76, 77, 79, 87, 94, 100, 101, 119, 120, 128, 131, 136, 139, 141, 144, 150, 152, 158; MPLA 92, 141, 144; *Operation Carlota* 31; UNITA 75, 87, 141, 145, 149, 154

Aoun, General 146

Aquino, Corazón 82, 83

Arab-Israeli dispute 9, 13, 28, 35, 100, 101, 109, 119, 121, 132, 139, 141, 142, 143, 145, 146, 150

Arab states 110, 121, 123, 126, 143

Arafat, Yasir 132, 143

Argentina 32, 94, 103, 122

Arias, President Oscar (Costa Rica) 144

ASEAN states 122, 143

Asia 11, 26, 27, 30, 36, 59, 100, 126; *see also* countries

Assam 146

Asunción 94

Austro-Hungarian Empire 26

Azerbaijan 34

Baker, James 69

Bakhtiar, Shahpur 84

Balkan states 19, 122

Basic Principles Agreement (1972) 154, 167-70

Basque country 85, 146

Batista, Fulgencio 30, 84

Batmunkh, Jambyn 112

Beirut 69, 87, 146

Belgium 26

Berlin 34, 109

Bhutto, Benazir 94

Bishop, Maurice 40, 41

Bolivár, Simón 53

Bolivia 29, 32, 80

Bolshevik Revolution 102, 115

Botha, Pieter 94

Brand Reports (1980, 1983) 155

Brazil 22, 32, 56, 74, 77

Brest-Litovsk 132

Brezhnev, Leonid 14, 15, 17, 97, 100, 101, 103, 110, 111, 112, 113, 115, 116, 117, 122, 129, 137